SOLVED
The Mystery of Life

Writings and talks of
VERNON HOWARD

Compiled & published by
NEW LIFE FOUNDATION
Pine AZ 85544

(928) 476-3224
Web: www.anewlife.org
E-mail: info@anewlife.org

Selected works of
VERNON HOWARD
compiled and published by
New Life Foundation
under license.

First Printing 1995

ISBN 0-911203-37-0

New Life Foundation
PO Box 2230
Pine AZ 85544
(520) 476-3224

INTRODUCTION

What you are about to read comes from a very high place indeed. It is for all who feel there is something missing in their life, for anyone who has wanted to know what life is all about.

Have you noticed how many so-called solutions really solve nothing? Are you getting sick and tired of all the lies? Well, here's good news. This book will help any self-honest person who wants to know the truth.

Vernon Howard makes everything perfectly clear. He will explain mankind's problem and its solution. You will discover fascinating insights into human nature that you never heard before. It's all here for you!

For example, everyone wonders about the difficult question of what to do with evil. *The Mystery of Dracula* explains why Bram Stoker's novel has been so popular ever since it was published. You will discover how evil forces torment everyone, an issue very much connected with our daily lives and with everything occurring on earth.

This could be the most important book you ever read. It will open new doors and supply explanations you've been looking for all your life. You will discover answers your heart longs to hear.

Work hard to understand what you're about to read. Let these principles shake you awake. Invite Truth to do for you what you haven't been able to do for yourself. And you will be forever grateful that you did.

Table of Contents

Chapter 1

The Eternal Creative Principle

Let me tell you what I like about New Life. We explore here and become introduced to a principle that we didn't know before. We certainly didn't know it as children or perhaps as young adults. We are introduced to a principle that is so different, so strange to us that at first we can't understand what it's all about. I want to tell you what it's all about now so that it will become very clear to you, so clear that it will be a part of your daily life.

To do this, think of the world five million years ago. Think of the universe two million years ago, a thousand years ago. Think of the huge planets and the suns and the stars and this world, which was in one stage of evolution or other. But they existed. Let's pull a figure out of the air and say this world here that we are living in existed say a million years ago. There were no countries and the continents were different.

A million years ago the world was different and the planets were different and the stars were different. They change. Just in our lifetime, we can see a change in the physical world that we live in. Maybe the Mississippi River is now ten yards to the west than it was when you were younger—something like that. Over the billions of years, everything is changing.

You change. How many of you looked like you did now as you did when you were eighteen? *(Laughter)* Ah, just one or two of you, I know. *(Laughter)* All right, so you change. How many of you think you are going to be as nice looking twenty years from now as you are now? *(Laughter)* How many of you don't think you are good looking now?

This is so profound! Everything is changing. You are changing, the world changes, the planets change, the rivers change, everything changes. But, here is why I'm glad there is New Life Foundation. We can know from more than just our intellects that the Principle, the Power, the Force, God—let's call it the *Principle* for now. The Principle is always there. The Principle that makes Mars appear and a billion years from now disappear. The Principle makes a certain physical body appear here on earth in 1920 or 1960 or whatever, live for awhile and then disappear. That physical body that has a name with clothes of a certain color and all that will disappear. But do you know that with *consciousness*, you can be a part of the Principle that causes planets to appear and disappear? Do you understand what it means that there is no death?

Look, there's appearance and disappearance of the Mississippi River and of the social conditions in the United States and every other country. Conditions change, the universe changes but something is in back of the changes that is eternal.

9

That is, there's no way you can get rid of the Principle that causes something to appear and disappear. It is greater than the appearance and disappearance, right? There has to be something in back of it and there is.

There is something in you that wants to live forever. There's something in you that doesn't like the idea of going away and not being anymore. However, because we human beings are in a stage and state of evolution, we don't know how to think correctly toward that urge to continue life forever. We make the mistake of thinking that the appeared person is eternal life. You want your body to keep going. Even if it is a hundred and fifty years that isn't enough and it isn't. To live for 2,000 years wouldn't be enough. You'd be worried about the 2,001st year, right? There is something in you that can be developed, that understands that your unity with the eternal Principle is what's in back of your yearning to live forever.

So what difference does it make that the physical form changes. This is not a rationalization now, this is not an attempt to try to feel good by finding an intellectual explanation. No, never, never, never lie, never deceive, never rationalize. Never look for hope. Abandon all hope until only the facts are left. Now we've got that out of the way.

You will eventually understand that your physical form is not important. It really isn't, but you think so because it's all you have. When you have something higher, then you understand that the Principle of creation and destruction is what you really want. That is what eternal life is all about, the knowing that when this physical body disappears, there's life beyond that. Of course there is. There's something that created this physical life and then allowed it to go away. And that is the Principle that you are always tied to but don't know it. That's why you are afraid of dying.

Oh, how sad. You're your own creator of your own petty, miserable, sick, little existence. No wonder you're afraid. You say, "Maybe I can take pills and live for another five years longer. Maybe people will help me and I'll get more money."

The Principle of eternal life always has existed, time-thinkers. When you don't identify yourself as a creator, when you don't think in time anymore or identify with your physical self or experiences—your petty, wretched little world—when you no longer call that the creative principle, the whole thing collapses. The whole question disappears of what's going to happen to you after death. You don't ask the question anymore.

What is to disappear? See, as long as you want to continue on your own terms, you're going to worry about not continuing physically. Then you know, through your hard inner work, that the principle of creation is the same thing as the principle of destruction.

Well, the young peach tree grows up and

11

after a few years the peach tree goes away. Doesn't God create another peach tree? See, you want to be a special peach tree. You want to be the only peach tree and have the biggest peaches in town that everybody admires.

Don't you want to live longer than a peach tree? Don't you want something more than a temporary existence? A peach tree goes away. The physical body goes away. You're worried about the continuance of that, when you can be with the Creator of everything. When you are with the Creator of everything, *that is eternity.* I once told you that you were never born and you never die. Can you connect that with what you just heard? When were you born? There was no *you*—you were never born. There's a *physical* you, but no *psychological* you coming into existence. People did that when they gave you a name. And you believed it. You believed in the name and thought you had to build that. If you were never born, which is a fact, you can never die, which is a fact.

What is life then? The life is what is behind the creation of all human beings, all planets, all oceans. Who created that Pacific Ocean? Did you ever think about that? It is a pretty big place. Did you create it? See, you want to be a creator of your own little petty happiness, for example, which is what wrecks your whole life, right?

I am glad for New Life because we can continue to study what we have studied just now, that we can be above life and death. We can see through life and see through death. The Creator of the universe is willing and eager for you to transcend your mind and your egotistical life in which you think that you started your own life. Then there is no you who fears coming to an end, because you see through the whole hoax.

In summary, *the Principle, the Creator of your life is eternal.* God did not put you into this world and give you a name and give you a few experiences for you to hoard like a miser and try to cling to. God did not give you that life—you did. And everyone else in your life helped you to build that false life. God put you in this life with a certain awareness, consciousness, to be developed, to understand. And the one thing you can understand is that you are not who you think you are. When you know that, birth becomes meaningless, growing old becomes meaningless, death becomes meaningless to you. You know that you are not simply a created creature who has a temporary existence and is afraid that that existence will come to an end.

You know that you are a part of the eternal creative Principle.

• • •

Chapter 2

Mystery Stories for Winning Happiness

Solve the mystery of yourself—and solve all else!

You may enjoy a mystery story, but no one likes bewilderment toward his own life. Lack of self-knowledge causes discomfort. But that happily means that by winning self-insight you also win self-ease.

A detective on a police force might have to travel thousands of miles to collect clues to solve a case. You have it much easier. You can stay where you always are—at home with yourself—and solve life. You are both the mystery and the detective who finally explains the mystery.

You discover who you really are by first understanding who you are not. You are not your collected opinions, beliefs, habits, experiences, defeats, pains. You are a timeless Spiritual Self, which you will discover for yourself with lasting delight.

All your questions about life will be answered. Here are examples:

"People seek but never find happiness. Exactly what is happiness?"

"For one thing, it is to not do what evil people try to trick you into doing."

"Are women at the mercy of men?"

"A true and spiritually awake woman has

absolute authority over a wrong and spiritually asleep man."

"Truth seems so hard on people, as if they have nothing good. What about the virtue of gratitude?"

"When a man expresses his gratitude he is merely announcing his availability for more gifts."

Each story contains many valuable spiritual lessons for your inner-development. So when reading, be aware of your mental and emotional reactions to anything you read. Keep paper and pencil handy and write down these special impressions. You will sight all kinds of interesting responses. Some will feel cheery and encouraging, others will make you nod with agreement, and still others will arouse your curiosity. Write down your reactions and insights in a single sentence. Number them. Here is how your list might start:

1. Safety resides in a place higher than my present level, so I will seek the higher.

2. Negative thoughts are self-damaging, while spiritual thoughts are self-healing.

3. Friends may pretend to care for me, but Truth alone is really loving.

Read each story several times. Continue to add to your information. Every once in awhile do nothing but slowly read and think about your list of discoveries. You will see them more and more turn into accurate and kindly guides for your personal daily life.

Anyone living in Spiritual Reality has no fear of evil spirits or evil human beings—which are the same thing. Inner invisible wickedness, which controls the person, explodes hatefully outward to cause fear, heartache, violence, crime. But there is nothing at all scary or mysterious about evil— not when you really understand it.

These stories supply the light of insight, which no darkness can enter. Now you are safe— now and forever.

Using *Mystery Stories for Winning Happiness* is an entirely new method. It combines the natural human love for a mystery with the deep human yearning for self-newness. It makes self-development a lot of fun. So cheerfully begin to investigate life's mysteries. The solutions are just ahead.

MASQUERADE PARTY

The immense room was noisily alive with the masquerade party. The costumes were colorful. Robin Hood saw the Princess approaching him. Her face was worried. He loved the full year that she had been his girlfriend. The Princess was pretty and energetic.

"An evil spirit is here tonight," she softly informed. "It's masquerading as one of the guests. It's whispering sly suggestions into people's minds that they will have accidents. It's working. A few minutes ago a man was struck by a car in the parking lot. Earlier, a woman was hurt in a fall."

Robin Hood squeezed her hand and smiled tolerantly. Her interest in demonology amused him. But sometimes he wondered why it attracted her.

"It could be Jack the Ripper," she stated as she glanced around at the whirling dancers. "Or maybe Dracula or Frankenstein." Coming closer she lowered her voice. "It gains control over people by fiendish repetition. It whispers accident, accident, accident so often they feel compelled to obey its sinister suggestion. So they walk right into what they fear—an accident."

Later, Robin Hood was standing alone, watching his own thoughts with curiosity. He smiled as he caught himself searching the crowd for the three suspects. He asked himself, "Which one is possessed by an evil spirit whose dark scheme is to cause an accident, accident, accident?" Wandering around, he located and studied Jack the Ripper, Dracula and Frankenstein. Standing close to each he tried to feel their psychic radiations. A faint suspicion arose in his mind.

He thought it would please the Princess to hear about his detective work. He walked along the edge of the hall, his mind heavy with thought. Several waiters approached, carrying a large table on their shoulders. He saw something slip, felt a hard blow on his head. As his mind faded out he glimpsed the Princess hurrying anxiously toward him.....

In the ambulance on the way to the hospital his mind cleared. A flash of insight entered. There *was* an evil spirit at the party, and he saw its cunning. It had stolen her heart. She had found a new love. That's why the evil spirit possessed and acted through the beautiful Princess.

THE CHANCE

The classroom was crowded with Truth-students of all ages. They listened with great interest as the Teacher discussed the need to become aware of unconscious wrongness inside. He remarked, "It's what we don't see that hurts." As the lecture ended the students reacted with understanding and appreciation.

"I will now take a few questions," the Teacher invited. "Who will start?"

A middle-aged man raised his hand. "Sir, you said that everyone has a chance. What does that mean?"

"Would *you* like a chance?" asked the Teacher.

"Yes, I want it more than anything else."

"You can have that chance. Please stand."

Nervously, the man stood up.

"I wish to ask you a very simple question," the Teacher explained. "Do you have concealed evil inside you? Yes or no?"

The man showed shock. "Well...I'd have to think about it."

"My question is," the Teacher persisted, "do you have concealed evil inside you? Yes or no?"

"I'm..." the man hesitated. "I'm not sure how to answer that."

"I will ask the question once more," said the Teacher. "Do you have concealed evil inside you? Yes or no?"

The man shifted uncomfortably and protested, "But that's such a strange question."

"For the fourth time I will ask you the same question. Do you have concealed evil inside you? Yes or no?"

"Yes."

"There!" exclaimed the Teacher. "Now you have a chance!"

CATCH THE DEVIL

The storm outside only made her more painfully aware of her own emotional storm. Glancing at her watch she thought, "Time to leave. *I must find out.*"

Driving slowly through the rain, she reviewed everything. Tired of the emptiness in ordinary religion, she had started upon her own spiritual quest. She felt close to an important breakthrough, but needed an answer to one vital question. She repeated, *"I must find out."*

As she parked in front of the building she felt nervous over meeting the Teacher. But when seated opposite him a few minutes later she felt relieved. That was because *he* was pleasantly relaxed. He invited her to begin.

"Please," she said. "I must know something. It's a missing piece in my personal puzzle."

"Please ask your question," he urged.

"Does the devil exist or not?"

"He exists as a temporary idea but not as a permanent Reality. I'll explain. When you think of the devil, what do you really have? Only a thought. Now, if it remained only a simple idea no harm could come to an individual. But the idea of a devil gets wrongly mixed up with self-reference, fearful imagination, a hypnotic attraction to danger, and other harmful states. So now the careless person is taken over and controlled by this directionless mass of wild energy which is called the devil. This is the cause of all human violence and suffering."

She asked, "If there was no devil *in* me there could be no devil *against* me?"

"That's right. The devil can't exist without you, without your unseen cooperation."

"How can I stop creating the devil?"

"Catch him in the act of trying to move into your inner home, as when he tries to enter with anger or gloom. Your awareness gives him no place to live and grow. All this will be explained in detail in our classes which start soon. Meanwhile, practice...."

She did. Later that day she went grocery shopping. A glass jar accidentally fell off a shelf and smashed at her feet. She was about to react with guilt and irritation, when she suddenly re-membered. She watched the devil trying to take her over, which prevented it.

"Devil—I've caught you!" she exclaimed.

She knew she had made a sensational spiritual breakthrough.

THE TOURISTS

As the bus entered the downtown parking lot the Tour Guide spoke into the microphone. "Ladies and gentlemen, we hope you are enjoy-ing this tour, to which you were sent a special invitation. We are about to make a final visit."

The Guide escorted the forty passengers into a busy government building, then to one of its rooms. "It's a courtroom!" a woman squealed, while the others expressed surprise and delight. They settled quickly into the seats. A door opened and the front of the room was soon occupied by a judge, jury, lawyers, clerks. A deputy sheriff stood to one side with folded arms.

A nervous male defendant stood up and faced the judge. "You have been found guilty of invisible crimes," the judge declared. "Your weakness taught weakness to your children, your cruelty tormented your wife, your constant anger made others believe that anger is a good and necessary reaction. Your sentence is to be pained by your own evil spirits until you permit Truth to make you a sane and good human being. You may leave."

21

A murmur arose from the astonished tourists. Someone whispered, "Punishment for *invisible* crimes? Who started *that?*"

A woman with a worried face next stood before the judge. He stated, "You are guilty of the invisible crimes of vicious complaint and cruel sarcasm, which lowered the happiness-level of everyone on earth. You are sentenced to suffer from your own devilish nature until allowing Truth to save you from yourself. You may go."

The judge handed down several more sentences for the invisible crimes of revenge and hypocrisy, then called for a recess. The Guide instructed the passengers, "Please return to the bus."

As the bus rolled forward the Guide spoke into the microphone. "Ladies and gentlemen, you have just witnessed a stage performance in a theater, with professional actors."

The passengers gasped, some with laughter, others with relief. A man shouted, "Thank heaven it was *only* a show. Keep me out of a court where you can be punished for wrong *thoughts!*"

The Guide told them, "People *are* punished for their evil thoughts, but few realize it. Everyone has an inner courtroom—judge, defendant, verdict, punishment. A man's punishment is to live with his own hideous nature. Truth will rescue him from himself—upon sincere request."

A passenger asked, "Why did we receive invitations to the tour?"

"Someone thought you should take it."

THE STATUE

He looked up as his secretary entered the office, set some papers on his desk, and hesitated.

"You have something on your mind," he pleasantly told her. "Please sit down."

Shyly and gratefully she did so. "Sometimes," she started, "I see you standing alone near the west fence. You seem to be studying something in the city park across the street. Maybe you're just relaxing a bit by watching the games and the picnics. I hope I'm not intruding...."

"Not at all," he put her at ease. "Like to solve the mystery of the studious boss? Come along with me. We have a few minutes before lunch."

They were soon in a position next to the company fence which gave a clear view of the park across the street.

"See that statue?" he asked.

The girl observed a statue of a famous hero of history. It was tall, solid, impressive. The face was strong and decisive.

"I come here often to take a good look at it," he told her. "It serves as a useful reminder."

"Reminder?" the girl wondered.

"Of the total insanity of society," he explained.

"That madman kept millions in terror and bank-rupted a nation. Now he's a hero to his very victims. There should be a sign on it that reads *Statue to a Psychopath.*"

The girl replied, "I've suspected that sinister fact for a long time. I'm relieved to hear some-one come right out and say it. I understand why you must come here alone."

He nodded. "You bring these horrors out into the open and the demon-worshippers will tear you apart. Maniacs love maniacs."

They watched as a man stepped in front of the statue. He looked up in admiration, saluted and walked away.

As they turned to leave he sighed and said, "Do you know where that man is heading? Straight for the lunatic asylum. But it will be disguised as something else. The lunatic asylum will be called a business office or a social club... or a happy home."

PRAYER MOUNTAIN

Seated at his desk, the reporter studied the large photograph of the mountain. Called Prayer Mountain, it was located in a distant country. Millions of worshippers from around the world visited it yearly to kneel at its base and pray up-ward to its peak.

"Strange," the reporter thought to himself. "Millions pray for peace but war comes. They request happiness and get misery. I'm going to investigate this puzzling contradiction."

It was a swift flight which soon brought him to the base of Prayer Mountain. Passing through the thousands of worshippers, he began to climb toward the peak, which he finally reached.

Then he saw it. A tall robed figure, his back turned, stood with arms upraised over the worshippers below. Then, as if sensing the reporter's presence, the figure slowly turned and lowered his arms.

The reporter gasped.

It was the devil! He stood there with a mocking smile. His eyes burned darkly.

"So now you know," said the devil in a strangely low voice. "Now you know who they are really worshipping. Me!"

The reporter said, "And I know why they pray for peace and go to war."

The devil waved downward in contempt for the worshippers. "Those cowardly hypocrites—they get all the horrors they ask for. *I* answer their prayers. I know what they really want. They don't want peace and goodness. They want *me*. It's *me* they really love. They pray to their own sickness, calling it heaven!"

The reporter nodded. "There's no other answer to the terrors on this earth. Human beings have gladly placed themselves under the curse of their own ignorance and stupidity. You trick them into walking in darkness while calling it light." The reporter paused, then added, "But aren't you afraid that I'll expose you?"

The devil's mouth twisted with laughter. "You think those praying sheep down there will believe you? I've fooled them for centuries. Nothing will change. I know my own."

"But a few may listen."

That shook the devil. Shocked, he stopped laughing. "The few," he muttered, staring at the ground. "That is what I always fear—the few who will listen and awaken...."

As the reporter returned to the base of the mountain he passed a group of worshippers who had just arrived. They were fighting over who would get to pray first.

THE GLIMPSE

Seated on his black throne in hell, the devil glared angrily down at the three trembling demons before him.

"A year ago," said the devil, suppressing his rage, "I sent you up to earth to destroy a particularly dangerous enemy. Well, he's still healthy and active. Thousands have heard him expose my tricks, and I don't like being unmasked." The devil tapped his throne with his forefinger. "You'd better have a good explanation for your failure."

The first demon quivered. "Please, your Satanic Majesty, we tried *everything* to lure him over to our side. We used the popular bribes of wealth and power and fame. He just ignored us and went back to reading his Truth-books."

The devil scowled. "Amateurs, all three of you."

The second demon raised his hands, palms upward, in a pleading gesture. "For six solid months we concentrated on trying to make him hard and bitter over the cruel treatment he had received as a child. But he refused to fall into hatred and self-pity."

The devil's manner was contemptuous. "You spent all that time—and he's still up there showing people how to escape our clutches."

The third demon was politely defensive. "Please don't blame us. We even offered him a series of exciting mental movies in which he was the world's greatest lover or athlete or whatever he wished to be. To show his gratitude he tossed out both the movies and us."

Shaking his head, the devil spoke with quiet fierceness. "I sent idiots to do the work of demons."

The devil's mood suddenly changed. He leaned back on his throne in silent resignation. The three demons peered up anxiously.

Breathing heavily, the devil finally spoke. "Don't you know the real reason you failed?

Don't you know why you will always fail with that enemy? I've been sitting here listening to you, hoping to avoid a certain conclusion which I must now face. The real reason you failed to defeat him is because...because...*You can't make him forget his glimpse of Truth.*"

THE CLIMBER

He sat at his office desk on the twentieth floor and admired the Climber some more. The Climber was older than he, and occupied his own office in the company. He knew that the Climber's brisk manner and prompt decisions would take him to high places in the business world. He wanted to be like him, so he used every chance to be with him, hoping to pick up some of his charm.

Later that day, when returning from lunch, he saw the Climber enter an office on the first floor. His curiosity was aroused. Their company had no business on the first floor. He prepared an excuse for making contact with the Climber, then entered the office, which was unoccupied. But he heard voices through the next door.

"In exchange for your services to his Satanic Majesty," a stranger's voice said, "you will be given great wealth and public authority and respect. But what have you done recently for *us?*"

He heard the Climber reply, "I've carried out every order of the devil to cunningly lie and deceive, while outwardly appearing to be a decent man. I assure you I haven't forgotten the main order to destroy while pretending to build."

His mind refused to absorb what it had heard. Shuddering, he quietly left and returned to his desk. He stared unseeing at the business papers. His mind whirled dizzily with the incredible thought—*the Climber is a demon in human form, employed by the devil!*

Later that day he had to deliver a report to the Climber, who greeted him with his usual enthusiasm. Not returning the smile, he set the report on the table and quietly looked at the Climber. The Climber appeared baffled, as if sensing that something was wrong but was unwilling to face it.

"Listen!" The Climber's manner was serious but excited. "Want to go places in this world? Success guaranteed! I need a partner in some very special work I'm doing. I know how much you admire me, so we'll work well together. Meet me tomorrow morning on the first floor, the office with the red door."

He said quietly, "I was there at twelve-thirty today."

The Climber's face twisted strangely. His eyes seemed covered with slowly circling dark smoke. "So you know," he breathed....

When arriving for work the next morning his desk was cleared, except for the notice which discharged him. As he left, the Climber was standing at the exit, a faint smirk flickering around his lips.

"You know," he said to the Climber as he passed. "You've taught me what I *don't* want in life. I don't want misery masquerading as success. It's nice to be free of you."

The Climber's smirk faded and he looked lost.

THE CHAIN

The Truth-lecturer had a confident manner and a pleasant face. He began, "In tonight's study of demonology we will concentrate on one special point. Hatred for Truth acts like a chain that ties the Truth-hater to the Truth-teller. A Truth-hater is possessed by a vicious demon who keeps him reminded of the person or place where he first heard spiritual facts. He can't stop thinking about it. Sometimes a Truth-hater writes hate letters, which, by the way, my secretary calls nut notes."

The audience smiled.

"This constant contact with Reality is a source of torment to a Truth-hater," continued the lecturer, "but his domineering demon won't let him go."

A hand shot up in the audience. It revealed a man whose eyes burned with deep hatred. "How come," the man demanded, "Truth doesn't rescue the sufferer from his torment?"

"There is no way to get through to those with whom there is no way to get through."

The man shook with anger. "If hatred is his torment, why does he cling to it?"

"Hatred supplies a strange and fiery pleasure to his egotism. The vibrations make him feel alive and important, but it is false life. His only chance is to let go of his hatred without asking what will replace it. Healing Truth will take its place, but he will know this only by first releasing his demon."

Shaking his head in contempt, the man snarled, "You said that hatred is a chain that ties the hater with the Truth he hates. Give me proof."

"Proof? You yourself are the proof."

"Me? In what way?"

"How long have you been attending my lectures?"

"For thirty years."

MADNESS NEEDS NO MOTIVE

Her boss simply called her in and said, "You are young and pretty. My two sons are returning after a long absence. Please allow my older son to escort you to the company party tonight."

She laughed. "Don't I get a choice?"

He smiled back, then grew serious. "I must tell you something. My younger son has been diagnosed as demon-possessed. He appears normal, but his demon flares up suddenly when feeling rejected. Then he attacks and smashes whatever is nearest. We'll keep an eye on him at the party."

31

As arranged, the older son picked her up in her country cottage. They chatted pleasantly while riding back to town. She was impressed with his handsome features and good manners. Once he stopped on a lonely road to adjust her seat for comfort. She thought about mentioning his brother but decided against it.

Arriving at the party they were greeted by her boss. Drawing her aside, he pointed out his younger son. "Avoid him," he warned.

But the unexpected happened. While she was alone for a moment the younger son suddenly appeared, gripped her elbow and breathed, "Don't resist." As he forced her outside she glanced anxiously back, hoping they had been seen. But soon they were isolated in a dark garden. "Let me explain my father," he pleaded, coming closer. She froze with fear.

"That's enough!" The command shot out of the darkness. Seeing it was her boss, she ran to his side, gasping with relief.

"You stay out of this!" the son shouted, but they were already hurrying back to the party.

She felt safe as the older son started to drive her home. Most of her cold fear had faded. After awhile the car suddenly slowed down. She glanced inquiringly at the man. His face had turned hard and inhuman. The car stopped. Turning slowly he asked, "Why did you reject me from the very start? Just like everyone else, you rejected me. Why?"

She trembled with horror. Her hand quietly slid across the door, searching for the handle.

"It's locked," he said.

She screamed and threw herself hard against the unyielding door. At that moment the driver's door flew open and the younger son appeared. His voice rang out with authority. "Leave her alone! Stop *now*...."

Later, she and the younger son were seated in a cafe. He explained, "My father deliberately deceived you by matching you with my brother. My father and brother are equally mad with the same demonic spirit. I didn't know about my father until tonight. If you wonder why it all happened, it's very simple. Madness needs no motive for exploding. It explodes just because it's a bomb."

THE TERRIBLE SECRET

Down at the huge office he was known as the Information Officer. People came to him when wanting to know something about anything. Outside the office he also knew something. He had discovered a terrible secret. It came to him because he possessed a rare power. He had the power to penetrate human hypocrisy and see human beings as the smiling devils that they really are. By long and hard study of human nature he had learned the terrible secret.

On one occasion he was part of a crowd outside a large building when several famous world leaders walked out. They did what he knew they would do. Each slyly glanced around to make sure he was on television, then deliberately acted out various impressive gestures and facial expressions. He knew that several of them had brutally tossed political rivals into jail. Others profited from organized crime. He looked at one of them and thought, *"He* is a world leader?"

Another time his duties required his attendance at a convention of several groups who claimed to be promoting international cooperation. He saw groups sneering at and fighting other groups in an attempt to seize power. One group broke into a rival group's office and destroyed the records. And, of course, they lied about it to the police. Leaving the convention he asked, *"They* are making things better?"

On a third occasion he attended a holiday picnic at a huge state park. He observed and noted: *A drunken, wandering woman cursing with sex words...a fistfight between two city officials... someone screaming his camera had been stolen... vandals carving up a tree...witnesses laughing and enjoying a shocking car accident.*

He knew the world was inhabited by demon-possessed human beings. And he knew that this was no mere slanderous figure of speech—that it was a hard and observable fact. They *are* what they *do.*

Over the years he had never informed anyone

of his terrible secret. He sensed why he had to remain silent, but could not put it into words.

One day the Information Officer was at his desk when the girl across the aisle came over. They liked each other.

She was troubled, but managed a smile. Hesitating briefly she asked, "What's wrong with this crazy world?"

He gasped. Never before had he ever been asked *that* question. His mind repeated, "What's wrong with this crazy world?" He reviewed his terrible secret.

Then the full horror of it all flooded over him.

No one would ever believe him.

• • •

Chapter 3
Inside the Lunatic Asylum—Society

Human society is one gigantic lunatic asylum. But the inmates don't know they are lunatics, which is why they remain lunatics.

Society's lunatic asylum includes people both inside and outside the stone walls of a mental hospital. Those on the inside are simply more obviously out of control. Those on the outside are simply better actors.

The cause of a crazy world is crazy people. What else? But everyone thinks he is the exception. He, of course, is a perfectly sane and decent person, while it is others who are evil. This delusion is part of his madness. Only awareness of lunacy can cure it. Only consciousness of being all wrong can make anyone all right.

No society or government can behave any higher than its Lunacy Level. The Lunacy Level is the average level of mental illness in any group or country. So since society consists of individuals, the only way to lower the Lunacy Level is for a self-honest individual to stop lying about his spiritual illness and allow Truth to heal him. But there are so few who place Truth above egotism.

Senseless people always react with the same lies when exposed by sanity. They are never original in their frenzied attacks against Reality. For example, they accuse Truth-tellers of being negative. But it is the lunatics themselves who are negative. Their own shrieking hatred proves it. But with their usual dishonesty they refuse to see this fact.

There is only one truly positive force in the universe. It is God, Reality, Truth.

One reason people remain inside the lunatic asylum is because they cannot understand *mental crime*, which is invisible. They can only understand visible crimes like murder and robbery. But for every crime observable with physical sight there are ten thousand mental crimes which remain unseen by spiritually asleep human beings. This includes intimidating people with cruel threats, misleading others with false information, taking advantage of human weakness for personal profit. It also includes the invisible crime of constant self-deception by which an individual keeps himself in mental chains. All of this is part of the lunatic asylum.

Few people ever see the full horror of the human condition. Why? Because the lunatics outside the walls have all conspired to call each other sane.

You can do much better. You can live as apart from human madness as a mountain cabin is apart from a noisy city.

Imagine a man who hears about a buried treasure, which he eagerly seeks. Then he hears about a second treasure, then a third, then a fourth, so he turns toward each of them. So he wearily seeks, changes directions, but never finds.

People desperately seek the treasure of wealth or security or love, growing scared and confused as the prize eludes them. But the weary wandering can end. It ends when the individual finds a *new kind of treasure, that of spiritual sanity.*

You are about to read some spiritual mystery stories. Be an alert detective. There is a rich reward for your capture of the many truths contained in each story. The reward adds up to a new and free life.

Proceed as follows. Read a story several times. This gives you the full impact of its deeper meanings. Then, at the top of a piece of paper write: *LESSONS FROM The Evening News,* or whatever the name of the story.

Next, list as many lessons as you can find in the story. The lessons can cover many topics, such as freedom from angry people, spiritual insight, methods for inner healing, self-reliance, seeing through human hypocrisy.

Number each lesson and keep it short. Here are examples:

1. Insight into human nature supplies safety in human relations.
2. It is possible to live in this world and not be part of its lunacy.
3. I cannot fear a situation that I really understand.

Add to your page as new insights come to you. Review them often. Put these truths into practical practice during your day.

The Director of the asylum, whom you will meet in the stories, represents sanity and wholeness. The Director knows a great secret—that only the spiritual can deliver health to the human.

FROM THE BALCONY

The Director of the asylum and a new assistant stood on a low balcony overlooking the assembly hall. Below them dozens of men and women chatted, socialized, stood at the snack counter.

"Look at them," remarked the Director, "and never forget the first rule of this place. No one is what he appears to be. Everyone wears a mask, trying to appear nicer or wiser than he is. Look at them down there. They've played their stage roles so long they no longer know they're onstage."

The assistant nodded. "Self-deception is unconscious."

The Director gestured downward. "Glance around. Among them is a vicious psychopath who led his former country into a war that slaughtered millions. Can you spot him?"

Gazing around, the assistant ventured, "The tall man next to the table?"

"No," the Director replied. "The man next to him—the one with the charming smile. Try again. Find a lunatic whose paranoid persecution destroyed the mental health of an entire family."

"The man in the corner?"

"No, the woman to the left. It was her own family. We have a roomful of Truth-haters and degenerates of every kind. You think that's too strong, don't you?"

The assistant reflected, "It's worse than I thought."

"It's always worse than you think."

"And now they're your problem."

"No, not mine," said the Director. "We've been discussing the *visitors*."

THE OBSERVER

One man in the lunatic asylum was known as the Observer. Everyone called him this because of his habit of sitting quietly and patiently observing the other inmates. While the others engaged in friendly chats or helped each other in small tasks, the Observer watched quietly and took notes. His written conclusions filled dozens of pages.

One afternoon, wishing to test his discoveries, he walked over to one of the men. "Sir," said the Observer, "I notice that you eagerly give loads of advice to everyone on any subject. But isn't it a fact that all you really have to give is childish nonsense which you pass off as wisdom?" When hearing this, the man's body shook with rage, which the Observer promptly noted on a page.

The Observer next approached one of the women and stated, "I notice that outwardly you appear to have an innocent and spiritual nature, but aren't you really a religious hypocrite?" As the woman's face contorted with fury, she snatched up a religious book and hurled it at the Observer, who promptly jotted down a note.

The studious inmate then placed himself in front of another man and said, "Sir, you often boast of being a bold adventurer to faraway places whom men admire and women love. But I see you as a liar and a fake." With a snarled curse at the Observer, the man stumbled back and away. The Observer added a third conclusion.

Retiring to a corner of the hall, the Observer reviewed his new notes. After several minutes he nodded his head in satisfaction. Then he added another note which read, *"Why did each of them explode with rage? Simply because I told them the truth about themselves. Their hateful reactions gave them away. Only the guilty are afraid."*

Looking up from the page, the Observer was thoughtful for a moment. Then he made a final note: *"Maybe I'm in a lunatic asylum and don't yet know it."*

Standing off to one side, the Director had watched everything that had happened. He understood the conclusions reached by the Observer. Turning to his assistant, the Director commented, "You know something about the Observer? He won't be here much longer. Do you see what is happening to him? He is going sane."

RESPECTABLE PEOPLE

The woman sat across from the Director's desk and said, "As I explained on the phone, I'm writing a book on hypocrisy in high places. Thanks for your aid."

The Director opened a folder. "These should help. All are a matter of public record. Like some samples?"

The Director pulled a newspaper clipping from the folder. "Try this sample of human respectability. This man mailed sixteen anonymous hate letters to a large church. They were filled with blackmail demands and threats of violence. He was caught when he carelessly mentioned a club he had joined. He turned out to be a highly praised religious leader who saw the church as a rival to his power. He had a family, local admiration—a very respectable member of society."

The Director held up another clipping. "Here's a woman who founded a crusade dedicated to ending world hunger. She gave hundreds of lectures, collected millions of dollars, and occupied a luxurious office. One day a shipping clerk looked curiously at the destination of a truckload of food. They found she had been sending food to her own private warehouse for black-market profit and for her own home use. Another honorable social leader."

Closing the folder, the Director remarked, "You may think these are exceptions. Not at all. They are simply the ones who were exposed."

The woman nodded. "There must be millions more."

The Director said, "People don't refrain from crime because they're decent, but from fear of getting caught. Remove the police from the streets and nice and friendly neighbors would rob and rape each other like something out of World War II."

"Why do people remain sick?"

"Because they refuse to see that other-injury is the same as self-injury."

"Are those two people still here?"

"They never were here. The man now holds an even higher position than before. The woman still has thousands of devoted followers."

The Director gestured toward the open window. "They are out there...those nice, respectable people...they are out there destroying the world."

THE BUSINESSMAN

A businessman was driving to the edge of the city to attend a conference. A short distance from his destination his car broke down. Looking around for a phone to call a mechanic he sighted several large buildings surrounded by a white wall. Believing it to be an exclusive country club, he walked toward a nearby back gate. Entering a building he found himself in a large room which appeared to be the lobby. It was active with people whom he assumed were guests, secretaries, clerks, repairmen.

Not seeing a phone, the businessman wandered around, looking for someone to help him. Suddenly, out of the corner of his eye he became aware of a man hurriedly approaching him with an anxious face and manner. The man gripped the businessman's arm and quickly led him into a nearby office.

Indignant and bewildered, the businessman snapped, "What's going on? Who are you?"

"I'm the Director," the man replied. "And do you know the danger you're in—especially in *that* room?"

"Danger?" the bewildered businessman asked. "From what?"

"From just *being* here," the Director answered firmly. "Don't you know what you've stumbled into? You're in a lunatic asylum."

After a moment of stunned silence the businessman protested, "But...but they all look so normal."

"That's precisely the danger," the Director breathed. *"They all look so normal."*

REALIZATION

As she sat in the small room in the asylum she thought about it again. She knew the exact day she had realized that she was a lunatic.

The first small clues came after the breakup of her marriage. There were waves of aching loneliness and resentment, followed by guilt and bitterness. But there was something else that struck her curiosity with great force. There was not just the pain, but also a clear and detached view of the pain, just as if it were happening to someone else.

Later there were a string of boyfriends, with the usual quarrels and accusations. And again she had the curious experience of being furious toward the world while also realizing how much fury was inside her.

Then came the great explosion. She was approaching her car at the supermarket parking lot when a gang of punks wandered by. "Hey, lady, want some pop?" one yelled as he tossed a half-empty bottle at her. She ducked so that the bottle only glanced off her shoulder, but that was enough. She exploded with a scream of rage so fierce that it even scared the punks away.

That night at home she realized what she was inwardly—a raving lunatic. She knew that a sane mind could not possess all that hatred and suppressed violence.

She quietly informed herself, "Only a lunatic would continue with this self-torment. I'm going to do something about it."

The Director of the asylum had helped a lot. She was grateful for his explanations of her condition. He had said, "Everyone is a lunatic, but few want to admit it as a first step toward recovery. So congratulations on your positive attitude." He had explained how recovery is helped by virtues such as self-honesty and a wish to learn.

So as she sat there she felt good about herself.

"Good night," a voice from somewhere broke through her wall of thoughts. "See you tomorrow."

She glanced at the clock, walked to the parking lot and began the drive home. She smiled as she realized something. This was her fifth year as secretary for the asylum—also her fifth year of climbing toward personal sanity and happiness.

THE BOARD OF MENTAL HEALTH

There was once a local Board of Mental Health. Its three men and three women had been appointed because of their qualifications of being prominent in politics and business. One man had been appointed because he had once read a book from which he had quoted at the right time and place: "The very heart of mental illness is egotism, a wish to appear important."

One morning at city hall they decided to be of help by visiting the regional mental hospital. During the drive, one woman announced that her husband had just been promoted to supervisor of his company's paint department. Another member promptly proclaimed that her husband had been asked to fly to Montana to correct a company problem. A male member remarked a few minutes later that a few friends had asked him to run for mayor. He did not name the friends.

The board members were greeted by the hospital Director, who asked how they planned to connect their visit with aid toward the recovery of the patients. "None of us has ever seen mentally ill people before," one man quickly explained. "Our very study will help. Be assured we are not merely curious." The others nodded vigorously.

The six started the tour by wandering among the patients out on the spacious lawn. An attendant appeared who was having light fun by calling out "Free candy" and handing out donated chocolate bars to the patients. As he passed the six members, one woman asked if she could have a couple of bars for her granddaughter. When given, she quickly dropped the candy into her purse and started talking about the well-kept grounds.

While visiting one ward they decided to be helpful by showing personal interest in a long-time inmate. When asking him about his earlier years he replied with ease. Then the six members fell into exchanging details about their own earlier years. When the patient walked away, none of them noticed it.

They concluded their tour at exactly noon, which made it natural for them to be invited to lunch at the cafeteria. One male member called out jokingly to a passing inmate-waiter, "Hey, you're not going to cheat me out of dessert are you?" But the waiter knew he wasn't joking.

Back in his office, the Director phoned the new guard at the front gate. "The members of the local Board of Mental Health are leaving," he stated.

"Don't let any of the patients slip through."

The guard asked, "How do I tell the difference?"

The Director gazed wearily out a window. "I really don't know," he sighed. "I just don't know."

THE RULER

You think there is no justice in this world? Well, there is. But it's a strange kind that few people like to think about.

Take the case of the Ruler, and I'd better tell you right now how he acquired that name. When the young man was first employed by the government his boss told him, "Your task is to enforce laws regulating mental institutions. And since you must make them *measure up* you can—ha!— think of yourself as a *Ruler.* Get it? You are the royal regent of regulations. Ha!"

The young man not only got it but liked it. Not a bad start for a nobody. So over the years he ruled the asylums with fierce authority. He made laws and suddenly changed them. A rule issued on Monday was contradicted by another rule issued on Tuesday. He furiously scribbled regulations that no one could read or follow. With great glee—and angry threats—he tyrannized wherever he could. After all, he was the Ruler.

One day the Ruler was promoted. His way of doing things earned him an appointment as district judge.

But in less than a month the horror of it all dawned on him. His own laws were now passed on to him for final decisions. He had to face his own monstrous creations. He was forced to try to make sense out of nonsense. So in daily terror he had to sit alone and strain, shake, agonize, hate, fear....

You will usually find him sitting all alone out on the asylum lawn. He won't let anyone sit next to him—he's afraid they will mention the law.

All this happened because he overlooked a certain natural law. It has several names, such as the law of cause and effect, or retribution. They simply mean you get what you give.

So there is justice after all. And obviously it is also a warning to people like the Ruler.

THE EVENING NEWS

A dozen patients had gathered to watch the local evening news on television. The opening scenes showed two cursing mobs hurling rocks at each other. The streets were littered with the groaning wounded.

The scene shifted to a hall in a government building where a fiery debate over the rioting mobs was in progress.

One speaker angrily denounced the brutality of the first mob, while praising the virtues of the second mob.

The next speaker furiously attacked the viciousness of the second mob, while defending the peaceful defense of the first mob.

A third speaker screamed for everyone to remain calm. He proposed that sixty-thousand dollars be spent to finance a committee to study what he called "This social misunderstanding." He suggested that his own poise and wisdom made him the ideal choice as chairman of the committee.

The scene moved to an aisle in back of the speakers where two women were battling each other. Shrieking and pulling hair, they fell to the floor together. They sat there for a stunned moment, then cried.

One patient seated before television in the asylum turned away for a moment. He caught the attention of the Director who was passing by.

Nodding toward the television, the patient asked, "Why aren't those wild maniacs in here?"

"They are," declared the Director. "They just don't know it. But plans are being made to build a new wall around the asylum. I'll recommend that they make it circle the entire town."

THE ATTACKER

In the asylum, the man behind the doctor's desk stood up and extended his hand to the reporter. "Please pardon this out-of-the-way office," he said, "but they're making repairs in the main buildings. I asked you to come here so we wouldn't have to compete with hammers and saws."

"No problem, doctor," the reporter assured.

"But what about the mysterious attacks here? How many—nine or ten?"

"A dozen. We call him the Attacker. The victims have been doctors, nurses, visitors, other inmates. He's always one thought ahead of his victims."

The reporter made a note. "What do you know about him?"

The man at the desk shook his head. "Very little. We have hundreds of possible suspects. You know what a big place this is with dozens of buildings, garages, basements. Lots of places to hide. I'm afraid we have a lunatic on the loose."

"How does the Attacker operate?"

"Very convincingly. By appearing harmless he gains their confidence. You know how gullible and suggestible most people are. Be pleasant to them and they think you're nice. Once they think they're safe they're not."

Said the reporter, "He sounds a lot like people on the outside."

"Of course. We all have cunning when it comes to self-interest. People on the outside attack invisibly, as with hateful thoughts. Our Attacker can be seen physically."

"Do you think you might identify him soon?"

"We don't know. The Attacker is cunning but not intelligent. Cunning is self-destructive while intelligence is self-elevating. Therefore neurotic cunning is also stupid. Can you think of anything more stupid than to be a self-harming human being? The Attacker lives from the stupid thrill of his dangerous game. Lure and strike. That's his sick excitement."

The reporter paused, then said quietly, "Doctor, aren't you afraid to be here with me? Maybe I lured you out here. What makes you think I'm a reporter?"

The man at the desk stood up. "What makes you think I'm a doctor?"

The reporter stared in horror as the man at the desk just stood there and smiled in a strange way.

DIARY OF A LUNATIC

She descended the library steps into the basement and searched among the dusty books. She finally found the book she wanted, which had a worn paper cover. In her six years as asylum librarian this was the first request for it, though the library was open to anyone inside the institution and even to the outside public.

Upstairs in better light she again read the title, *Diary of a Lunatic*. There was no author's name. Flipping the pages back and forth, she read with great interest, while her mind recorded gems of thought:

> *Like everyone else, I thought I was sane, but like everyone else, I was an unseeing lunatic...My greatest fear was exposure as the madman that I was...I began my search, discovering that the way out consists of the*

inner work of becoming aware of my fanta-
sies which I pretended were virtues...Very few
wish to become sane, but those few can
surely find their way out of society's lunatic
asylum....

Taking the book to the Director, she enthused, "This is so *different* from the usual dull and confused explanations. I'm absolutely fascinated."

The Director quickly absorbed the book's message and handed it back to her. "Only a sane mind could have written this," he agreed. "Take a good look at whoever requested it. You will likely see an unusual person, someone who really understands life. You may see someone who has risen above the intellect to the truly spiritual level of self-wholeness.

She hurried back to her desk, eager to see who had requested the book. Would it be friend or stranger? It was so rare to meet someone who preferred healing truths over sugary lies. But the note from her assisant had said only that the book would be picked up today.

As the afternoon passed she alternated between reading the book and glancing toward the entrance. Dozens of people entered, but none approached her desk....

"May I have the book, *Diary of a Lunatic?*"

She was suddenly aware of the voice speaking to her. Looking up, her reactions froze as she stared at the pleasant face.

"Oh," she finally whispered to herself. It's *you.*"

THE REVEALERS

It was Saturday afternoon, and the Director was about to deliver his weekly lecture. The asylum hall was crowded with patients and their relatives, staff members and the general public.

"I'll tell you a strange story," the Director began. "A skilled inventor created a pair of magic glasses which he called the Revealers. By wearing the glasses, he could see through human pretenses and see people in all their actual evil. The inventor sat in front of television and let the Revealers expose one human horror after another. A powerful reformer was revealed as a hideous monster whose only real concern was for self-glory. An international diplomat was discovered to be a leering fiend who loved to destroy. The inventor realized what a terrible truth the glasses had revealed—human beings are nothing but decorated packages containing hatred, greed, violence, lies."

The Director continued, "The inventor knew what would happen if an unprepared person were to look through the Revealers—he would collapse with shock and horror. So the inventor tried to hide the glasses, but one day they were accidentally lost. They were picked up by a group of people on a picnic near a lake. One by one the people looked through the Revealers—and one by one they screamed at the ghastly sights and fell violently to the ground. They revived, but were never again the same."

After silently studying the audience for a moment, the Director continued. "Ladies and gentlemen, those Revealers actually exist. In fact they are in this room right now, available to anyone with the courage to take them. But they are spiritual, not physical. Go through the shock of seeing human beings as the maniacs that they are. Tell the truth about human evil—yours and others. You will finally become a whole and healthy and happy human being."

The Director concluded, "Yes, this is the way it is in this hideous world. Will you look—and be healed?"

For a moment the audience sat there in stunned silence. Then they gazed uncertainly around at each other. And then each one lowered his head and seemed to be looking within, at himself, with eyes that stared and wondered....

THE ZOO

He was terrified. He was leaving the asylum tomorrow and he was terrified. They were out there waiting for him. They always were. And now he had to go back to relatives and friends and people who hire you and people who demand answers. They would pounce on him and make him feel stupid. The only thing that helped was something the Director had once told him: "It's not necessarily paranoid to feel that people are out to get you. That's an absolute fact out there in the big lunatic asylum."

Another time the Director had been even more blunt about human stupidity. "Half the visitors who tour this place are nuttier than the patients. Know the real reason they come here? Conceited comparison. They look at someone in bad shape and congratulate themselves for not being *that* loony."

But fear still gripped him as he wandered around the grounds. He could hear himself pleading to the world, "Please don't hit me again."

And then he met the girl. He didn't know where she came from, but she was pretty. He could see that. He realized that he must have somehow communicated his fears to her, for they were soon seated together and chatting.

She sighed, "People are coldly cruel and then lie about it."

"I know. They scare me."

"I used to feel like that," she said.

"But I discovered a mental exercise that changed everything. I often visited the city zoo. On all sides of me were ferocious beasts, but I knew there was no way they could hurt me. Why? Because I was smarter than they. I was human and they were animal. This helped me to see human society as a huge zoo—a zoo of beasts I need not fear. This started my thinking in the right direction."

He nodded. "I never saw it like that."

"Once you see people as animals they lose all power to scare you," the girl continued. "Take an angry man. You should see him as wild and weak—and that's all."

"That's interesting," he commented. "Pouncing people are scared animals."

She smiled. "I'm sure you've known someone who was a cunning fox or a smiling crocodile."

"And don't forget the vicious wolf and the sneaky weasel," he added.

They laughed and enjoyed each other.

The next day as he approached the gate of the asylum, someone called out, "Going home?"

"But first to the zoo," he called back cheerfully. "I'm going to become a lion tamer."

• • •

Chapter 4
The Mystery of Dracula
Part I

Here is something bright and cheery for you. If you will let these truths, these lights that you're going to hear tonight, enter you and become your personal guiding lights, you will have an inner experience that you've never, ever had before, an experience that will make everything new. It will make you new, therefore, it will make everything in your life different and refreshing.

What will happen to you as a result of loving Truth more than you love anything else is that you will become in command of a certain world. That certain world is the only world that you have to conquer. There's nothing that you can see out-side this door that you need to be the conqueror of. It's the inner world. It is the world of your life that we're talking about. That's the important thing to you, isn't it? You want to find out more about why you haven't conquered this inner world yet, why it has been too much for you so far and why every way you've turned, you have run into a blank wall.

So, it's good news to know that simple recep-tivity, getting yourself out of the way right now while you're hearing me and you're looking at me and I'm looking at you, now is the time for you to do something you've never even tried to do before: to get your old nature, the way you've always thought, out of the way so that something new can come in. There's only room for one thing. You can't mix darkness and light. Now, if you want the light that's going to change the kind of a human being you are, so that you're not subject and a slave to your own wrath anymore, to anything anymore, but are in complete command of the one world that you have to command, it can be done.

I'll tell you a little secret at the start. You see, God knows all about his world and he also knows about Satan's world, the dark world. Satan only knows about his world. Now there's significance in that for you. The significance is this: If you are on the side of what is true and you really have a spiritual life, you really have a soul because you've developed one through your work on yourself, then you're on God's side. That automatically means that you know everything about the dark side of humanity. You know all about those dreadful things that have been attacking you in the night. You know how afraid you have been. If you are on the side of light, then you know everything about light and everything about darkness. This means that a person who does not want to find Truth only knows about darkness and nothing about the light. Therefore, he can only live with that darkness, which makes him a very sad, a very angry, a very hostile and a very lost human being.

The explanation that I have given you is the good, cheery, bright, marvelous news. One solid truth that you allow to penetrate you right now can chase away a dozen problems. If you don't know that, then allow it to enter you so that you can prove it for yourself. Everything here is good news because it's all about learning.

The novel *Dracula*, written in 1897 in England, was an enormously popular success. Everyone was reading it. It made its author, Bram Stoker, a famous author almost overnight. Now, let's look at why a book about Dracula, about vampires, would so fascinate and entrance people that it became the best-seller that it was, and still is.

I will tell you why. The book *Dracula* was something new to the consciousness of the people of the day. What it did, primarily, was something they had been waiting for for a long time, and at last it came along. In the book *Dracula* were explanations. That's the key thought to remember as we go through this tonight. The book explained things for which they had never had an explanation before.

Now, everyone in that day and in this day had heard about evil. You've heard about Satan, you've heard about evil spirits. But have you noticed how difficult it is to know what an evil spirit is all about? And, by the way, if you did know what it was all about, if you really knew what it was all about, it would have no power over you. Now, look, let's be careful of what we're talking about. I said "evil spirits". What does that mean to you? Let me tell you what it has to mean to you. It means your bad temper. It means you being afraid.

It means you not knowing what to do and getting desperate and then insisting right in the middle of your desperation that you know what you're doing in life. If you know what you're doing, how come you're so miserable? And you are. Nobody knows that better than you.

All right, *Dracula* explained the following: when you read the book or see the movie about Dracula, that is invisible evil made visible, right? Here's a man who's going around with his cloak. They dramatize it, of course. He goes around with his cloak and you can see him in operation. Now if I say "Understand human evil," that's too vague; you can't grasp it yet. But if you see Dracula in a movie or read about him in the book, going around performing all the nefarious acts that he's performed, it becomes clearer to you, doesn't it? Evil, which was a word to you, a vague feeling, you can see going around. That's what attracted people to the book and made it so popular because they were beginning to understand something about evil that they could not understand before.

There is Dracula leaning over the woman in the bed—we'll talk in later talks a little bit about the sexual part of it. He's slinking around and he's biting people and you can visit his castle if you want. You can go inside and see all the dark secrets of his dark kingdom. As the physical moves around and operates, you can understand it. There's evil talking. Dracula is pure evil, is he not? Of course he is. There he is talking and you can listen to him and you can find out what he says and analyze it. You are now in a position for you to understand evil where you could not understand it before because the physical representation is so clear—and this is what the readers thought.

But the explanation went far beyond that. And I'll tell you, I want you to examine your reactions to the talk you're getting right now. I've been watching some of you and I've seen your facial expressions. I want you, from this point on—and you should have done it at the start of the talk—to notice what happens to you regardless of what I say to you. Nothing is more important than for you to get acquainted with yourself.

You think you already know yourself. You don't know the smallest thing about yourself, which is why you are so scared and such a slave. Now, don't you dare, for your soul's sake, for your life's sake, for your sake, push away anything that doesn't agree with your present concepts. That would be a very, very bad thing for you to do, to put it mildly.

All right, you've had some reaction to what I've said in the last minute. See what it was and don't identify with it because you are not that reaction. Ah! Now people who read the *Dracula* book can begin to understand something that is both enlightening and frightening at the same time. You know what it is? I'm going to put this to you very bluntly. You see how much you can take tonight. The reason the book was so fascinating and so scary at the same time was because people had their first insights into the fact that they were Draculas.

Well, Dracula is a symbol, a representative of everything that is bad, everything that is sneaky, everything that is evil, everything that needs to live off of other people. And the readers of the book—maybe some woman in London or a man in New York—would read a chapter, put the book down and go and look out the window of their house and they would see Dracula in action.

They would see the headlines of the war between two countries, two groups of people slaughtering each other and then they would hear their neighbors fighting, two people living together and spending their lives screaming at each other. The sound that you hear is only a small part of it. They're internally screaming at each other the rest of the time.

Oh, yes, down at the office, you know, the office intrigues and the petty jealousies and the ambitions to get the next promotion and all that. Ah! This story of Dracula that I'm reading is happening here and now! This isn't just in a history book or in a novel or in the movies. Dracula is here among us right now.

The majority of people turn away from seeing that because it's getting too personal. Don't you do that. You let this talk get as personal as it can be because that means health to you. "Oh, it's getting a little close," the people say, "to what I'm hiding inside myself; therefore, I won't finish the rest of the book or I'll criticize it in some way."

Dracula, summarized right now, was such a popular book and there's a reason why. He's such a popular figure because of many things; but, the one I'm concentrating on right now is that he reminds us so much of us and we can see it.

People don't understand—and I'm going to use several words in this—their own evil, their own stubbornness, their own egotism, their own vanity. They don't understand their own ignorance, therefore, they don't understand how they perform Dracula-like actions and drain other people.

Look, I said Dracula is here and now. This is a class in getting rid of delusions. That's why I want you to know that. I'm going to give you an exercise on it in other talks, but just for now I want you to ask yourself, "What impels me to be cruel? What impels me to be sarcastic and reject anything that doesn't fit in with my little pet theories about what life is all about and what I am and where I'm going?" Ask yourself, "Why am I so afraid?"

You will understand that you're afraid because you have not investigated the vampire, the Dracula in human nature, including your own, until you understood that there is only one thing in this universe that can save you from yourself, which is something that is not a part of yourself. You've been trying to rescue yourself.

How about these little things I've been talking about? How about a sarcastic spirit? How about that blasting out at someone, not so much with your mouth because you might get fired or someone might dislike you, but that blasting of another human being? Well, isn't that evil and isn't that what we're talking about? You see, when you say the word "Dracula" it should from now on mean to you what I've been describing. As a definition here it is: *invisible evil made visible in a humanized form.*

Let's see how you react to this! I want you to know that evil is *nothing but* evil. I want you to know that Dracula is *all* bad. I want you to know that anything that is not *for* God is *against* God. I want you to know that Dracula is against life. Every human Dracula on this earth wants to drain someone else in order to get a false feeling of life out of it.

I'm going to present something to you now that will further our understanding of the parallel between the Dracula story and the life we are living right now. When you read it, you'll understand what I'm getting at. The events and conditions in the story of Dracula explain many things in actual daily life.

Here are ten parallels between the novel
Dracula and in everyone's daily life:

1. In *Dracula*, Dracula's only perverted purpose is to sneakily invade and destroy as many individuals as possible. In life, every man or woman feels under attack by weird and diabolic forces which he can't explain to himself.

2. In *Dracula*, he can victimize only the weak and the ignorant and the foolish and the unspiritual. In life, everyone can recall griefs caused by one's own senselessness and egotism.

3. In *Dracula*, he is terrified by the light of day and is destroyed by its pure appearance. In life, evil is driven out of dark humans by the light of spiritual wisdom.

4. In *Dracula*, his successful disguise is to outwardly appear good and pleasant while inwardly he is a ferocious fiend. In life, think of some people you know who were at first all smiles and friendliness, but who later turned into the monsters that they really were. (That hit you, didn't it? Because you know people like that and you got foolishly involved with them because you didn't know Dracula when he came along.)

5. In *Dracula*, whoever is bitten by a vampire becomes a vampire himself. In life, a weak mind is easily lured and corrupted by promises, by false friends, and the bitter and disillusioned victim, in turn, preys on others.

6. In *Dracula*, he fears and hates God, goodness, and symbols of Truth. In life, with great slyness, evil humans try to destroy any appearance of true spirituality.

7. In *Dracula*, a vampire attacks when its victims are asleep or otherwise off-guard. In life, humans are spiritually asleep while dreaming they are awake and their ignorance is their danger.

8. In *Dracula*, he is an absolute abomination occupying a human body. In life, smiling psychopaths and hypocritical haters are far more numerous in society than society realizes.

9. In *Dracula*, he uses terror tactics to stun, shock, and subdue his victims. In life, demon-possessed subhumans use wars, financial panics, threats, scary rumors of all kinds to manipulate and wreck their human victims.

10. In *Dracula*, evil as represented by Dracula and his vampires is finally conquered by humans who are armed with inner rightness. In life, anyone who loves and lives with the spirit of Truth is protected day and night from both visible and invisible wickedness.

Once upon a time there was a village in the deep woods of Transylvania. Well, we've traveled there. Now some miles from this village was the vampire castle. That was the name the villagers gave to it because of what went on inside. And here's what went on inside at night with those vampires. I hope you know that I'm talking about human beings. Have you made that connection yet? You should have from what we've covered so far. I'm not saying a word that is disconnected from human beings, from people you work with and walk with.

The people in the village were attacked regularly at night while they were asleep by vampires who slunk out of the castle and came on down and bit them. This is symbolic of what happens to everyone in the world today because human beings are asleep spiritually, thinking that they're awake, thinking they know what they're doing with their lives. None of you know what you're doing with your life. You understand that, don't you? You say you know what you're doing, but you don't know what you're doing because if you knew what you were doing, you'd be a happy, free human being instead of an angry, frustrated, hostile human being.

Let me interrupt the story. Which are you, a happy human being, free, pleasant all the time? Or are you sour and hostile, always looking around for someone to blame and attack. I want you to take the lessons, what you're hearing into your life so that you won't be a self-divided human being anymore. Being good is the most practical and pleasant kind of a human you could ever be. You're not at all practical so far. And how many of you would call yourself pleasant? You're so unpleasant you can't stand living with yourself and you never tell that dark secret to anyone. That is part of vampirism, of the dark kingdom.

Why are we studying this? To get rid of the mess. You either want to get rid of the mess or you don't. What you do with this information decides the issue for you as a human being here on earth. Make the right choice for your sake. Not for my sake or anyone else. It's your life that we're talking about right now. I'm not talking to a mass audience at all. I'm talking to this gentleman and that lady—I'm talking to you!

I know you don't like it that way. I know you don't like to hear that you're part of the vampirism scheme. If I ask you if you are a bad person a lot of the time, you say, "Well, *some* of the time I'm a bad person." That's what we're talking about. Vampirism is not separate from being a bad human being who is cruel to your girlfriend. Or maybe you ladies have a sharp tongue toward men and you trick them. I don't know who is the cruelest, men or women. It's a tie and isn't it a shame?

The mayor of the village brought the villagers into counsel and he said, "This can't go on. We've got to do something about these vampires coming down every night and attacking us, the men and women, even the children. We've got to do something about it." So at the meeting the mayor said, "All right, I'm looking for volunteers to do certain work. I want some of you to get the equipment together for the trip up to the castle so we can get over the walls and get inside to put the vampires out of business. And I want this gentleman over here to do this. You're in charge of the torches." There's always torches in the village in a Dracula movie, aren't there? Then he gave assignments.

Now I'm going to tell you what people are really like. Let's see if you think it's like you or not. I'll let you be the judge. The man who was supposed to get the torches said, "I can't go. I have to go out of town for several weeks." He gave an excuse. The man who was to get the equipment together said, "Oh, I think it's wiser if I stay home and protect my family instead of going with you." One after another, all the villagers gave an excuse why they wouldn't be brave, climb over the walls and go get rid of the vampires. No one would help him. No one would go with him.

You know what the mayor said? This is what you want to say. This is what you must eventually say if you're ever going to be a sane, decent, good human being. You must say what he said, "I'm going anyway. If necessary, I'll go all alone." Someone asked him, "Why are you going all alone?" And he said, *"Because it's the right thing to do."* Why don't you try living by that rule once in awhile—or, better yet, all of the time. Do something because it's the right thing to do. But your trouble is, you don't know the difference between right and wrong. You never have. You've never known the difference! No wonder you have trouble being good and choosing what is right.

Well, where have you classified yourself? Are you the mayor or are you one of those cowards who, when the time came for deciding to stand up for decency and goodness, *for your own sake*, didn't have sense enough to know that to be good is to be good for your sake; because you've got the wrong entity inside of you telling you what is good and bad. It is lying to you and you don't have the intelligence enough to see it. It's about time you started seeing it so that you no longer spread evil into the world like everyone else is doing.

The mayor was different. He was unique. He lived by spiritual truths, not by a lying mind. As long as you have a lying mind you're never going to be a content, happy human being and you're always going to be afraid. You're going to be afraid of vampires, no matter what form they come in. The mayor said, "I'm going." The others stayed home. The mayor went to his house where his wife and two children were. They came out to the yard. He kissed them, they waved goodbye to each other and he turned and he walked all alone into the dark woods toward the vampire castle.

Not one of you has the slightest notion what it means to stand alone, to walk alone, to be brave, to be apart from the mad, sick, insane society that you live in. You're part of it. You'd better begin to learn what it means to get apart from the craziness of this world and not be in love with it anymore.

He went off. Days passed. A week passed. And they were all wondering what had happened to him. Did the vampires get him or did he get the vampires? It became the topic of conversation in the village. None of those cowards would say, "Let's go find out. Let's go up ourselves and find out and give him a hand." None of those cowards would do that! And that's the kind of a world that you live in. You'd better leap away from it, starting right now. Otherwise, the same thing will happen to you. I'll tell you about it in just a little bit.

A month passed. Finally he came back, battered and bruised, but alive and well. He reported that he had rid the castle of the evil vampires. And the vampires in that particular castle would not come to the village anymore because they were out of business. But he also reported something else that made them all a little uneasy. He said, while he was traveling around, he saw that there were several other castles out there and they were also inhabited by evil creatures, vampires and demons.

After he came back, something strange happened that no one could understand except the mayor, this one spiritual human being among a pack of miserable cowards. What happened was that the vampires from the other castles—they were invisible vampires you couldn't see—came down and they attacked the village again, all except the one man who was now immune, because he had set forth into the inner and outer adventure and conquered them. They could not harm him anymore. He was protected. He was protected by rightness, by his own goodness.

You understand, Dracula can't stand goodness. He can only stand what he is, which is darkness, which is evil. You had better investigate your own resistance to light right now. You're discovering something quite unusual. Do not let it upset you. Don't let it disturb you. Just say, "I want to know what it's really all about," and one day you will. That will be the greatest day in your life.

The vampires came down and because they were invisible there were no visible marks on the necks of the villagers, but do you know what there were? There were marks consisting of sour-spirited human beings, of irritable people, of people who couldn't have peace of mind under any circumstances, who were easily upset by any event. They had wild eyes and they didn't look good. They had bad health.

What I'm telling you now is that all the woes of mankind, all the lies, the quarrels and battling, everyone hurting everyone else, is because you are bitten by invisible vampires. What do you think is the cause of you being an unpleasant person? Something has attacked you and I'll tell you who it is. It's everyone you've ever met. You see, everyone is a vampire.

You never learned how to become immune to it because you refused to go up to the castle and fight for yourself. If you don't fight for yourself, you'll remain as you are. Now listen to what I just said, all of you. Don't forget this. If you don't leave and battle badness, evil, sickness, all that is represented by Dracula, you'll have to face the consequences of that. If you conquer Dracula, you will have conquered the one and only source—Dracula representing evil—of all your unhappiness and of all your stupid arrogance in which you know better.

Arrogance is one of the chief vices that prevents a human being from conquering evil and, therefore, living with peaceful good. And every arrogant man or woman is a terrified coward. Arrogance is a substitute for intelligence. The next time you see an arrogant person, just realize you're looking at a very foolish, stupid, weak, cowardly human being. He is nothing but that and he will continue to be bitten. By whom? I told you that Dracula is within. The vampires are within. Evil is within. Therefore, that foolish arrogant man who has no future, no real future, will be bitten by himself.

I want you all to do some work now and I'm going to give it to you. I want you to remember a simple phrase. *What if everything I did was to build strength instead of hinder it?* Just write it down in your own way, in your own mind. What if everything I did, everything I said, everything I thought was for the purpose of building inner strength instead of hindering it? Haven't you spent enough of your life hindering yourself, blocking yourself from becoming the kind of a human being that you could be? I'm talking to you about realities. This isn't just an airy lecture. This is getting very close to you and all of you sense it. There is not one of you right now who doesn't sense that you're feeling something you've never, ever felt before, and it's about time.

What if the whole world operated on that simple rule: Will what I'm doing now give me strength or will it stop me from being strong? What if every speech you heard was based on that principle? It would be a positive speech, wouldn't it? It would be a good speech, telling people how they must be strong. What if everybody in the world did everything they did with this simple rule: *Is this going to give me strength or is it going to keep me in my weakness?*

Weakness is stupidity. A stupid man is a weak man; a weak man is a stupid man. You understand, we have no strength of our own, none of us. We're talking about inner strength, about spiritual power. And at the start of the talk I told you that if you would simply welcome these ideas and let them begin to live in you and to guide you, then you would know absolutely, no matter what your age, you would know for the first time that there is something besides you in this world.

Now you don't know that. You're so self-centered and looking to yourself to save yourself, which can never happen. I'm urging you to have an authentic spiritual experience in using these Dracula and vampire ideas that we've talked about as one of the open doorways through which you can go and find something that is much, much higher than what you are now.

Let me repeat a thought. Being good is the only practical and truly pleasurable state you can ever have. Don't you know how miserable it is to be bad, with all the guilt and all the shame and all the hot emotions? You know what it means to be bad! To be bad makes you feel bad. If you want to feel good, be good. And now you have a whole course in just one evening on how to reach this goodness which will make you happy and free at last.

I'll read a few questions aloud and answer them. You might recognize your own question here.

Question: *You once used the phrase "Deceitful Dracula." How does he slyly operate to weaken our will to resist him?*

One way, and you can understand this, is for the world—which is Dracula, society is Dracula—to become an unceasing and overwhelming blurring machine. You know what a blur is? It's something you can't see clearly. You can't walk or drive in it because you might bump into something. Now, deceitful Dracula, which is evil, wants to blur your judgment of what is good and bad. More than half the time you'll choose bad and even when you choose the good, that will be bad, too.

So one of the ways he works is to introduce false reasoning into your life. For example, lying to you about something and saying that something is true when it's false and vice versa. Even if you get on the track of trying to understand the difference between truth and falsehood, he has his little games ready.

Remember the fact, the very simple but over-whelming fact, that evil uses lies as a chief weapon. When Dracula lies and deceives people he does it by concealing facts and maybe adding a little truth. Dracula doesn't want you to discover what is true and what is good, to know the difference between the two, because that will be the end of him. As long as you don't know the difference, you're going to side with what your egotistical nature says is good. Therefore, right judgment is fatal to evil.

How do you get right judgment? It's so simple. Let's see if you can start on it right now, to put yourself in a position where you'll always know the difference between good and bad. Just want what is good. I explained that earlier. What is more practical, what is more pleasurable than for you to be a good human being? Now, being a bad human being, you pay the price for that. So you're going to have to want something different. And you can be sure that all the dark, hostile forces in this world are going to try to keep you blurred.

What are you going to do to unblur your mind so that you can always take what is good over bad? I'll tell you. To learn how to distinguish between good and bad, you have to be in school. We're here to learn, to understand and that's what removes the blur and nothing else.

Question: *I wish I had the strength that goodness brings, but I don't. Everything I meet in life is too much for me.*

This is a question of power. I was reading an encyclopedia the other day and it showed these big cement aqueduct pipes so big a man could stand up inside of them. As I read the story about it, I saw the spiritual application. Always translate everything into a spiritual meaning, because it is very helpful to do this. Here are these enormous cement water pipes going from the big river to the big town and it goes over mountains and through deserts and storms beat on it. The people getting the water never have to worry about it getting to them, do they? Those pipes are strong, powerful—nothing stops them.

The nicest thing in this life is to know that you can go about your daily business, in your marriage, occupation, traveling or whatever, and know that the water of life will always be there. Just as nothing could stop the water going through the huge aqueduct, nothing can stop God from being your guide and your refreshment wherever you are, if that's what you want. It will reach you if you want it.

You can't go back to what you were doing before you heard this information. Sorry! Oh, I'm glad that you can't do that. This is it. *This is the turning point.* This is where you refuse to be a miserable, wretched little coward anymore. What is the reason those villagers wouldn't go up to vampire castle? They lied about it. They lied and they lied and they lied. They didn't go because they were cowards. Do you know what a coward can always do? He can start walking toward the vampire castle no matter how terrified he is, and that's what you can do. You can take these truths and be as terrified as you are.

You are terrified, aren't you? You'll call it by other names. Watch the lies and don't believe in them. That will only blur the mind and you'll bump into yourself more often during the day.

Next question: *Why do humans resign themselves to evil as it approaches? Why is there nothing more than a whimpering resignation?*

Because that's all you've ever done. Bad news comes. The factory's closing and everybody is worried and wondering where they're going to go next. Don't join them! That member of your household is putting pressure on you and you resign into what? Into tears? Into hatred? Don't do it even one more time! Don't resign like a weakling! Any foolish, stupid human being can resign when a challenge comes along. You're not going to do that anymore. You're going to right now take a new, fresh interest in your life. And it's about time on that, too.

You've never had a real interest in your life. All you've had an interest in life is grabbing and holding. What have you got? You got the man, you got the home, you got the activities, you've got the bank account and you're a miserable wretch. And that's why you whimper and resign yourself to the slightest challenge that comes along. God himself says you don't have to do that anymore. So why are you disobeying God whom you claim to want in your life? Why are you disobeying God when you collapse and bawl or get hateful when that little tiny challenge comes along?

I told you what to do. Take a new interest in your life. The old interest is wrecking you. You see, not a single human being on this earth of his human nature can help you. So you have no business relying on and hanging around lost human beings who only have a human nature.

They have no future and neither do you have by hanging around them. You better put yourself in a physical position where there is something more than human nature going on, where there is spiritual nature, where there's true righteousness going on, so that you can learn from that.

And last question: *Why do we cheer up and feel relieved at the end of the movie when Dracula is finally defeated?*

Because it's your victory, right? Haven't you identified with the hero or heroine? When Dracula is put out of commission, you now feel safe. All is well. And you say, "Ah, so there *is* a way to conquer evil." That's good! That's a moral lesson. There *is* a way to do it. Now, why don't you find out what it is?

And let me tell you that the exultation and pleasure that you feel when Dracula is conquered in the movies, is nothing compared to the second victory of you conquering the vampires and all the dark forces that are in your life.

Now, I want to make it clear before you go out of here. We've been discussing Dracula with his cape and his accent, his fierceness and his evil. We've been discussing vampires. We've been discussing the entire sick human situation, how everyone is bitten by vampires and becomes one himself. There is a way, the way of Truth in which all the considerable damage that has ever been done to you and from which you suffer, can be undone.

Again, I present to you the choice between you wanting to undo it or you stay as you are—and it will get worse as you grow older. It is fatal to go too far without making a decision for God and goodness because the time will come when you'll no longer be able to make one—you won't be interested in it. We want to catch you while you're still interested in saving your soul.

All this is bright and cheery. Only goodness, strength, virtue and newness can come from what you've just heard. Remember that. Don't let anything inside of you tell you anything different because it is up to its old tricks of lying to you again.

Oh, what a marvelous lesson this has been. We've been walking around in the Light, learning more about it by learning about darkness. *The more you learn about darkness, the more you learn about light.* And you gradually transfer yourself from dark to light.

Light is eternity. That eternity and that light is yours if you want it more than anything else. And if you're weak and if you're a coward, then keep studying. We'll show you how to be brave, one step at a time. This is your first step. There are many more. This inner adventure is lots of fun and very exciting. *And it's the only thing in your life that makes your life worthwhile.*

● ● ●

The Mystery of Dracula
Part II

The need for entertainment and recreation is a perfectly normal, natural need for human beings. We need to relax from what we're doing all day long at the workplace. We need to put ourselves in other positions inside of ourselves so that we become balanced human beings who are using all of our parts. For example, a human being who doesn't have a sense of humor is not properly using the lighter parts of him, which are equally necessary for a healthy life.

So, when you read Dracula and similar stories, I want you to know that it's just fine, it's nice to be entertained by it, to relax and enjoy the storyteller's skill, to study the characters and the scenes, to consciously be in a different kind of a world than the one you usually are in. For example, if you're in Dracula's castle, you're in a different place from where you usually are. However, you must be consciously in the castle and never lose yourself in the story, which means to respond wrongly from fearful emotions. You must be a reader of the story who is not a participant in it.

I want to talk to you a little bit right now about a wrong kind of spirit that inhabits human beings. Because we're going to talk about evil spirits, about possessing entities, and so I want to introduce you to one of them right now that you will find inside yourself. So you're now to look with new eyes toward this spirit I'm going to tell you about and see how it is a part of you. And you could use Dracula stories for seeing it clearer and get it out before it ruins you any further.

It's called the spirit of being contrary. Contrary. You know what the word means. It means something opposite. It means going against what you presently believe is right, going against your present lifestyle. That is, if someone gives you advice that goes against the way you want to think and live, you go contrary to it. You say, "No, that is not right," which is the wrong thing to do. Instead of being contrary, be perceptive. And related to a spirit of being contrary is a spirit of criticism. Don't they go together being contrary and having a critical, angry spirit?

Now on the surface it feels to you as if going contrary, saying "No, that's not right" is giving you security and giving you life and giving you a solid position on which to stand. It seems to give you a solid foundation. Wrong. It's sand.

And here's what you're to do. Here's your exercise in studying the contrary spirit. I want you to see that it owns you. You don't own it. That is, you're not in a right relationship with it at all. It's a slave and tyrant relationship. When you criticize, you had to criticize. You couldn't stop yourself if you wanted to. Now why am I bringing this up in this talk? Because it is one of those cunning, sly, sneaky Dracula-like characteristics that I don't want you to employ during the talk. Otherwise, you'll miss the meaning.

The spirit of contrariness wants to dominate you as you listen to what you're hearing this morning. It wants to be the one in charge of you and therefore, does not want anything that is contrary to that to take over. Being untruth, being false, it doesn't want Truth and verity and rightness to take over. Therefore, it will go on an all out effort to take over your feelings, to take over your responses, to take over your mind, so that you won't hear and learn, so that you'll stay exactly as you are.

Now you have a right aim, to not stay as you are, and now you know how to further that aim, which is to sit upright, spiritually at least, and watch a contrary voice trying to push away what you're hearing. Now, the contrary voice is the enemy. It is what is keeping you as you are. Therefore, your consciousness of it, your awareness of it sneaking in and saying "I know better than what that man is saying," seeing how it sneaks in must be your aim right here while you're listening to the talk. Otherwise, it will bite you and put you under its spell without you knowing it because you fell asleep and Dracula, that vicious vampire, was able to work on you even right now. So this means you have to be alert and awake right now. So do it. Come awake.

And don't sit here and listen with a dull, smug, satisfied mind, but with a mind that is alert to its own self-defeating behavior. You must catch Dracula the moment he climbs in that window and starts approaching the bed where you're sleeping. You get up from that bed, right now while I'm talking and you see him coming. Then you'll be able to hold up the cross of righteousness and he won't be able to proceed any further.

Now in the novel *Dracula* by Bram Stoker, one of the incidents is very descriptive of how evil is able to penetrate, how it gets inside us because we're not fully awake at all times. Come awake now. Jonathan Harker, who was the early hero of the story, went to Transylvania and from there went to the castle.

And he went there for a very legitimate reason. He was in real estate. And he was going to sell Count Dracula some homes or something in England. So he came there as a businessman. He didn't know anything about Dracula at all. He walked into a place where he didn't know what he was getting into. Sound like your life? You walked into the castle in Transylvania. Oh, and you had all those plans for making a profit, didn't you? What was the profit? So you walked right into it.

But here's one of the lessons in the early part of the story: Jonathan Harker comes up to the door and the door opens and Dracula is standing there. Now listen to this. It's very important spiritual psychology. Jonathan Harker, the gullible businessman, is standing outside the castle and there's the doorway and Dracula is right on the inside. You'll find what I'm talking about right in the story. And you know what Dracula said to him? Dracula greeted him and said, "Come in of your own will. Welcome. Come in of your own will." What happened? Living in spiritual sleep, Jonathan Harker stepped over the threshold of his own will into the dark, mysterious castle. *Of his own will.*

Now here he is, over the threshold, doing it voluntarily, stupidly but voluntarily. Now he's inside. And the moment he got inside, Dracula changed from a sober figure in front of Jonathan Harker to being very effusive: "Come in, my guest, we have things for you. And we want to talk business." He was very friendly. Now what's the symbolism of that? Once you surrender, the first step of a human vampire is to put you at ease. Because when you step over the threshold into the castle, you sense something wrong. You do, you feel it, gloom.

Ladies, haven't you been out with a boyfriend and he took you somewhere you didn't want to go? In your heart, you really didn't want to go into that bar, into that little weird place. You sensed something wrong, but *of your own free will you went anyway* because you were stupid. You didn't have the courage to just say *no*, not just to men but to *all* wrong invitations, where you sense you're in the wrong place.

He didn't sense it. He didn't have the intelligence to sense it. So Jonathan Harker stepped
in and the con game of making him feel safe and
secure began. That was his big mistake. Dracula
said, "Come in of your own will." Only when you
surrender your will are you a victim of the castle.
If Harker could have had spiritual values inside
of him, he could have stood there and looked at
Dracula himself and sized him up in two seconds.
And could look back and see the cobwebs,
which are symbolic of all that's old and useless.
He could have looked back and said, "Of my own
free will I am not going inside. Good day, sir. The
business deal is off. I don't want to discuss it."
And he would go back to the inn and from the
inn he would go back to England and could have
been safe. But no, he said, "Yes."

Now the scenario of scheming went into full
operation. Count Dracula got him up to one of the
rooms and said, "This is your room. I'll have
dinner for you in a little bit." When it came, it
was a nice dinner. Also appealing to the everyday instincts of people, he was in a nice room and
there was a library. He wandered around in it
for a little bit after dinner. And it still didn't occur
to him that he was in a wrong place physically.

When is it going to occur to you that you are
in a wrong place in your inner life and have no
business being there? It's hazardous for you to
be there and you had better get out of there fast.
We will teach you how to become extremely

perceptive to danger. And after awhile, that perception, that knowing will be operating twenty-four hours a day and there'll be no strain to it at all. There'll be no anxious looking around, wondering if you're in danger or not. When you ask whether you're in danger or not, that means you don't know. When you really know, you're completely at ease.

See, danger is ignorance; ignorance is danger. So when you're spiritually intelligent, you can look out at the whole world and know at a glance whether it is a wrong place. As you walk in and out of places and talk to people, you know instantaneously and have always known that it's a wrong place.

You're in the wrong place if you're associating with this world. You have a physical self and it belongs in this world. That's okay. That's how you communicate with this world by having a physical self. But you're in the wrong place psychologically and spiritually if you're afraid of it. When you're not afraid, that means you are only physically, but not mentally, a part of this sick world. You don't want anything from it. You have no business deals that are so overwhelmingly attractive that you fail to see the danger that you're in.

Isn't it sad and too bad that we never learn until it's too late, until the trap is sprung? That human being so charmed you by giving you your own room and dinner and putting the library books around to make it look scholarly and proper. Isn't it too bad that we never wake up until we wake up terrified? If you would learn to be intelligent, that wouldn't happen to you again. You would never voluntarily, of your own free will, step inside Dracula's castle in the first place. Stay out of trouble in the first place! To do that you have to be more intelligent than your greedy demands to make a profit. Work for that.

Jonathan Harker wandered around the castle and he tried one door to go to the next room and it was locked. The next door he tried was also locked. He tried a few more, and now the suspicion dawns that he had gone too far, that it was too late. He had passed over the line where he could never go back. That is, he suddenly realized with great terror that he was not a guest but a prisoner. And at that time, no doubt, he remembered the earlier conversation he'd had with the evil Count Dracula, how the Count's manner and the things he said had something abnormal about them. But there was the thought of that huge commission for selling that huge house in England. He refused to listen to the warning that was coming to him, and so do all human beings.

I told you that Satan has his warning system set up so that, if Truth starts to come toward a human being, he immediately begins his attack. God also has a warning system for you, but you don't listen to it. That alert, that warning system is going off right now. And what it's warning you about is to not be contrary, to see how you are saying that you are smarter than what you're hearing this morning. I tell you, yes, you are. A part of all of you, to one degree or another, is saying, "I know more than that." I warned you about thinking with a contrary spirit. You *don't* know more than what you're hearing.

You don't know anything at all. That's why you're in danger and that's why you feel surrounded by threats. That's why, if you don't listen to what God wants to tell you, you're going to rise from that nice dinner table set in front of you by Count Dracula and his vampires and you're going to wander away from those impressive looking library books and you're going to try the first door. And the terror starts there. Already you're worried, aren't you? And then you try the next.

Don't let it go so far that you try that first door inside and then the second and then the third, because if you do, if you go that far, you'll be in one of the worst states a human being could ever be in, which is to begin to call that dark, hideous castle his home, his pleasant home. And you will settle down in that dark place. You will say, "This is not bad. This is good." You'd do that to justify all your lies and your love of evil. You would do all that because you'd know you were trapped.

And I'll tell you this—which is always good news—if you don't go too far and you sense that you're inside Dracula's castle, you can always

get out by sending up a request, a prayer to something that is outside the castle. What's outside the
castle? Ask what is above it. That's it. You never
think of that because you're so tied up inside
yourself asking how am I going to get out? You're
asking yourself how to get out and it's yourself
that got yourself into it by crossing over the
threshold with the old greed, the old wish for the
profits and the honors and the glories of this world.

Don't miss the purpose of this life, which is
to be a human being who, even though you have
been tempted and lured and trapped—to be a
human being who refuses to join the enemy, who
says, "I'm not stepping over. I'm turning around
and going away from darkness." That is something
you can do. You don't have to listen to any assault on your free will. All you have to do is ask
God to be with you wherever you go. Then when
you go to the door of the dark castle and Dracula
tries to lure you in, it's no contest; he'll never win.

The reason you can win is because there is a
part in you that wants to be happy. No, you
don't understand what that means. But you do
understand what it means to be scared. Oh, how
you understand what it means to shudder. You
sense that whatever would be the absence of your
misery would be happiness. So you want something that is not the usual you and there are ways
to find it. That's what we are talking about.

Why is Dracula so popular? Why is he able
to lure them by the millions inside and trap them

in there and then bite them and drain them, drain them of their life so that he can live, of course? Dracula lives at your expense. Simplify that in common everyday existence. All human vampires live off of other human vampires, and the whole world is one mass of vampires. Everyone is draining everyone else. Now, don't say that's not right. It is right and you've got to see that it's right. If you don't see that it's right, you will be victimized.

Why is Dracula so popular? When the book came out, I told you, it was a bestseller and so were the movies about vampires (Dracula's similar creatures). They're very popular with people. They're fascinating to people. Why? Here's the psychology of it. All humans are insecure. They're weak, they're helpless, they can't think straight about anything at all. They wander around in a daze, just as you do. Now, in seeking relief from the pain of weakness, they look around and try to find something that is not weak, something they can look up to, a hero, a champion, someone who seems sure of himself. They look around in society and never find it because it's not there. Not having found the security in finding power in the world, they get even more desperate from it, and now that faculty called invention and imagination comes into play. An insecure man or a woman says desperately, "I've got to find someone who is stronger than me. I can't live this way anymore. It's too agonizing to be scared." I'm talking about you.

93

Dracula comes along. He stands up tall, he has his costumes, which are well put on in the movies— he's stately and he's a member of royalty. A man or woman looks at Dracula, symbolically speaking. Dracula can be a world leader. Dracula can be a man you met down in the bar. And so you say, "He seems to be different from me. I am weak and he appears to be strong." And so you attribute strength, wisdom, power to that other person, whether it's a public hero or that man, and you say, "Now I'm all right." Your evil has joined his evil and his fakery has joined your fakery. Now there's two sick, miserable people who have made a compact, an agreement with each other to pretend that both are strong. It's mutual lying. You are right, I'm right, let's tell each other we're right and everything will be all right. Now you've got two people, hand in hand, going inside the castle together.

So what I'm talking about is that when a human being does not seek to heavenly sources for power, he will glamorize and glorify Draculas and vampires in every form, and then comes the hero worship, the applauding of the political figure or whomever and saying, "Now I am safe." No. Now you've stepped even deeper inside of Dracula's castle. Aren't weak humans very popular when they're demagogues? You know what a demagogue is? I'll define it for you. A demagogue is a public figure who, either in his speeches or in his writings, can harangue the crowd, screams out lies and with great emotionalism gives people exactly what they want. He is a Dracula also.

Human beings look in the wrong places. They look on the level of this earth instead of looking upward. If they looked upward, it would occur to them that there is no point any longer in looking anywhere on the horizontal level. Looking there is only going to lead you eventually into the castle and down into the dungeon. That's where you'll live. And that is called the maximum depth of madness, of insanity. See this symbolically, please. Anyone who lives in the depths of his own nature is mad and down in the dungeon, which is very heavily populated.

One of the questions that came to me had to do with why women are attracted to Dracula. What is the sexual symbolism? There's quite a bit of it in novels and especially in the movies, the way the female vampires dress, or Dracula bending over the bed, for examples, are sexual symbolism. Instead of sex, he takes their whole life away from them.

Women, I'm talking to you now, in particular, about your mistake toward a man. Aren't you weak, ladies? Doesn't your femaleness yearn for maleness? If you're normal, it does. If you're abnormal, it doesn't. If you're a normal woman, your femaleness longs for maleness, for strong, right maleness. You've been so disappointed, haven't you? You haven't found it. Dracula then becomes the substitute. The man you met down at the bar, that con man just wants to go to bed with you, ladies. He wants to bite you sexually, so to speak. That's all he wants from you.

Ladies, as you stood on the threshold, you did not look up to Heaven and ask God to tell you what's going on inside of you so that it could stop. Instead of praying to Heaven, ladies, you looked at Dracula standing in the doorway. He seemed so sure of himself with no hesitation at all. Well, of course! Evil *never* has any hesitation! It's all out! It's a blast! It knows what it wants. It has no doubt about what it wants, which is your destruction. Of course it looks confident. You're so far away from understanding the whole spiritual story. You don't even know that Dracula—standing in the doorway, seeming so authoritative, like someone who can give you something—you don't know that he's one of these cowards we've been talking about. If you knew it, you wouldn't do it.

Your wish to find a strong man has been terribly thwarted. In your confusion, you'll settle for anything that you can get. Take a close look at what you've got. I'm talking to the ladies now, know that you have made a very serious mistake. You didn't know that you could have understood what was going on at the threshold. You could have understood it. But instead of taking understanding as your first choice, you took something called hysterical hope.

Ladies, how many men have you gone through? Men, how many Dracula idols out in this world have you gone through? Dracula can also be a physical object, you understand, something you want really badly, something that represents security to you on a very low level of human existence. A gun represents security. A big wall around your house represents security. People put up big walls and barred windows around their house to keep evil out. But because evil is spiritual in its origin, it flits right through, doesn't it? It goes right through the wall and gets inside of you.

How strange, how pathetic, how tragic that human beings only think in terms of physical safety. That's because they don't understand the need to see that inside they need safety. You think that if you can keep the burglar away or the thug away, then you'll be all right. Why don't you understand that you have a need for a spiritual wall, that you need a spiritual weapon, which is the only thing that's going to conquer all these various and vicious vampires that have lured you across the threshold.

I want you right now to start thinking, living, feeling from the spiritual viewpoint. The spiritual is everything. Your desires are nothing. Your opinions as to what's going to make you a safe person are nothing. I want you to put the two words "spiritual power" foremost in your mind.

Write them on a piece of paper so that the very next time you come up to the castle, that horrid, horrible, hideous place inside you, you cannot be tempted, you can't be lured. You'll stand there and know that you have come to the wrong place. How nice it is to know that you did not get into trouble this time because you never stepped inside in the first place.

I tell you that this will become a very real and very clear experience to you. After it's all over, you said "No," you did not go inside, you did not agree with those people, you didn't give them your money, you didn't give them your body or whatever. When you get back home, because you have spiritual power as the only guiding light in your life, just while you're walking around your home twenty-four hours after saying "No," it will suddenly occur to you that there is a wisdom that is a billion miles higher and sharper than yours. And that wisdom came to you at that moment of crisis and decision while standing at the door of the castle.

God spoke to you. God came to you because you didn't want to get trapped and hurt anymore. You agreed that there is a wisdom that is higher than your greedy wish to make a profit, to get glory or whatever. You agreed that you yourself are not the source of your own wisdom. Therefore, you abandoned your source of self-wisdom, which is your muddled mind and allowed something else to take over. It's a very interesting experience and you'll have it lots of times. You'll realize the reason you don't get into trouble ten times a week like you used to is because you're not walking into it with your own wish and ideas of what you need, of what you should have, whether it's a man or a financial profit or the applause of other people. Then your whole life is guided by spiritual power. And, oh, what a different day you'll have.

Now you're free of Dracula. Now you're free of his enticements and lures. Never again can he get you, no matter how powerful he seems or no matter how well disguised he is because spiritual sight can see through every darkness. Just like the spotlight out into the darkness, you see everything out there and you understand. Now you stay in your own home, your own spiritual home.

Now you are really safe and you know you are.

• • •

The Mystery of Dracula
Part III

Question: *Please discuss the sign of the cross. Why is a mere symbol so all powerful against the hosts of hell?*

The elevated cross sends an absolute message to all the Draculas of the world, a message that

Draculas and all evilers must obey. The order is absolute and the order is this: You shall go so far and no farther. When the cross is held up, evil can recognize goodness, not that it wants goodness, but it can recognize it. Evil knows that it's different from what it is. And when it sees the cross held up, which is symbolic of Christ, of God, of true spirituality, Satan himself must obey the message to halt.

You see, Satan knows when a soul, a spirit has put itself under the protection of God and is holding up the cross. That's it. The individual has said, "I'm on the side of God, not on your side." And it understands, to it's enormous rage and frustration, that there's no argument. There's nothing to talk about.

There's something to talk about when the individual holds up his gold, or holds up his priceless possessions. Then there's something to talk about, because Satan realizes the trickery in a human being, that he wants to strike a bargain. When I said "holding up his bank account," whatever, that means that the eviler wants to get into an agreement with Satan and get Satan's rewards.

When you hold up the cross of rightness, that means you have put yourself on the side that Satan can't cross over into. No way at all. If you stay on that side, the whole matter is settled and he knows it.

Here's a little extra side thought on that. When

you hold up the cross, you say, "I'm going to be on God's side." Satan knows that this is where he has to stop. And then, listen to this. He goes into a rage. He goes into violent hatred. Why? Two reasons: One, he loves hell, which is rage. He wants to feel more of himself. When I'm talking about Satan, I'm talking about Satanic human beings. That's what they do. And Satan also knows, in his rage, one thing that he's always known, but he comes face to face with it and coming face to face with it, he loves the rage that he gets. Satan knows that he is not God.

There is one thing that the Devil must try to prove. Look for this in human beings and don't think I'm talking about way down in Hell. I'm talking about right here. The one thing that a contrary person needs to try prove is that he is God, that he's right, that his position is the right one and all other positions are wrong.

Now do you understand why you get mad when you don't get your way? You are a part of the Satanic complex which wants to be a God unto yourself. That means you worship yourself, and you know inwardly you'll never be able to prove it. You fly into an insane rage of one kind or another when you come into a major confrontation with what is true and good, and you are defeated. A person who goes into too many of these confrontations and is defeated ends up in Dracula's castle, an insane human being. Only the cross can restore and maintain your sanity.

Question: *Why am I so fascinated with darkness, movies about the Devil or unearthly creatures, and find it so easy to give my attention to tragedy and destruction and find it hard to attend to things of the Light?*

Why are we so fascinated with evil? Because we're fascinated with ourselves. Well, are you good inside or are you bad inside? Now, badness can mean simply confusion. Isn't it bad to be a person in chaos inside of yourself? You're fascinated with evil in Dracula because you are Dracula. You'll do anything to have self-reference. You'll do anything to get and stay involved with yourself. And the more painful the better! You want big Draculas, not little ones. The more you can swim around in the raging storm of your inner nature, the more you think you can block out the fact that *God is God* and *you are you.*

You even want to take your agonies and your desperations as signs of being someone: the great martyr, the great sufferer, that person who's never known anything but being cheated and swindled by everyone else. You're fascinated with evil because you're fascinated with yourself.

Now, instead of being fascinated with evil, become a student of it. Those are two directly opposite states. Become a student of evil. Well, look how we've come full circle. How many times have you been instructed to examine and study yourself? To study yourself is nothing but studying evil. If you think that isn't true, you tell me what goodness you have. You tell yourself right now how you're a good person. If you tell yourself that you're a good person in any way at all, you will be lying and deceiving yourself. You'll be lured by Dracula across the threshold of the castle, and then you'll go down into the dungeon.

Let me summarize it. Please try to get this. There is no entity, no person there to be either good or bad. Don't identify with either state. Don't describe yourself as either state. Then you say, "Well how will I know who I am?" Your mind can never know who you are. It can only distort and keep you in the dark castle.

When you rise above your mind, when you're living with the Spirit of Truth, you will know who you are without ever talking about it, without ever speaking about it. Now you know who you are in the wrong way. There is a right way to know who you are, which does not include any need to describe it. There is no desperation. Right now, you're pretty desperate to hang on to all your present positions because they tell you who you are. Even though you get knocked down by other people and you get into great problems in life, that is a part of your whole identification system. This means that your problems must continue because they feed you false information about your identity.

When you are no one at all, then you are someone different who doesn't have any need to describe who he is. The Spirit knows what it is, God knows who he is, and you as a human being can know who you are, as long as *you* don't try to know.

Question: *Dracula disguises himself in the form of many internal bats which drain my energy and time, which could be used for real self-elevation. Please expose one of these bad bats.*

There was a wax museum that had figures of great historical people of the past and they had a poll to see who was the most hated of all human beings in history. You always have to have Hitler there, of course, and Stalin; and they also had Dracula. Dracula won as the most hated human being of all. Hitler and Stalin were real. Why do you suppose a fictitious figure, a nobody won first prize? Why do you love to hate Dracula? Because you're saying that you're not him. Dracula, by tradition and by act and by nature is evil. Now, because you are not a child of God yet, you try to get your feeling of goodness by hating what you call evil. Dracula is evil, and if you hate Dracula who is evil, that makes you good, right? Unright. There you go again, getting an identity. I must be good, I hate badness.

It is badness to hate badness. To be a hater of any kind is to be one of the vampires in the castle. Will you drop your identity? Let's talk about hatred just a minute. Will you drop your identity as a hater? Will you drop the thrill that you get from it? See, what is more draining to you yourself—and to the people who, unfortunately, surround you when you're in a hateful mood—what is more draining than hatred? Isn't it a theft of energy that could be used for growing up, for becoming spiritually mature?

Everyone likes to slap the label of evil onto Dracula and other monsters like that so that by comparison, you can be good and you can be righteous. It does not make you good, it does not make you righteous. Only God is good.

Question: *Why do people like to read vampire stories and yet keep the inner meaning away from consciousness?*

We covered that and we'll do it again. The deeper meaning in Dracula is that you're all mixed up in his activities. Now, who wants to face that? See? We always come back to the same thing that when we begin to examine evil, it is always the other person who is evil. So we block out of our consciousness the fact that we're living in a bundle of neuroses, wishing to drain other people, to take from them.

Now, I want to tell you an evil that you have never identified as an evil, and from now on, you're always to think of it in the way I'm going to give to you. Insecurity, to be insecure, is deep, dark evil. Why? You take it as a virtue and you even brag about it. You like to tell people how insecure and how scared you are. That's you, an insecure person. When you feel insecure, you keep yourself in a very evil state, which is simply a state that's apart from God. God is perfectly secure. You can be perfectly secure as long as you don't want to be an insecure person.

When you are an insecure person, half the time you will feel yourself to be insecure and the other half of the time you will falsely feel yourself secure because you won first prize in the dance contest or because someone complimented your new dress or because you got a little advantage over someone or won an ego victory. Then you feel secure. Your "I" says, "See, I exist because I felt something." True spirituality is without the dungeon emotions like hatred.

Question: *Since evil is sly and sneaky, how can we get smarter than it is?*

Evil is like the wind. You can't see it, but you can see the results of it. If you were out in a wet, windy street, the wind might blow you into the river and you'd know that the wind blew you there because of where you are, because of what happened to you. You can't see the wind but you can see the results of it.

As an exercise until the next class, when you find yourself in a bad location, either internally or externally, in an uncomfortable position, I want you to know that evil got you there. Now you canbegin to see it, you can begin to understand it better. There is a cause for your feelings. There is a cause for the results that you get in your life. They're invisible and you can't see them, but you can see the results.

106

What is the total result internally of you living your life up until this moment right now in this room? What has been the total result? A wreck, an unhappy human being and one who is always arguing to keep yourself in your wretched position in the dungeon of the castle. The Truth comes up to the door of the dungeon. It comes up and has a key and it tries to toss you the key, and it does toss you the key and you, in your anger and hatred, kick it aside into a dark corner of the dungeon. This is exactly what is happening and nobody knows it.

Just the two talks we've had so far could have liberated the entire world if it came and wanted that key. They don't want it. The majority of the entities inside of you don't want it. You've been kicking it aside. Oh, how sad.

There it is. You could have the cross. You could hold up the cross which represents purity, which represents total authority over this sick world. You could have that cross and you could be carrying it around with you all the time, very easily, very casually, because God is carrying the cross for you. You could have it in front of you wherever you go and no evil would dare to approach you. But you don't do that now. You don't have it there now. It knows that you're without protection. It knows that you didn't choose the cross above all else. It knows that you chose you and your way of thinking.

Your lack of the cross, of carrying it, is what

causes you to be so angry, so furious, so arrogant. That is evil! You're suffering from the evil of your arrogance. A large part of you during this talk and, in fact, all talks is always arguing. You would rather be contrary. Too bad for you.

What we want to do is to put you in a position where you always have that cross every day, wherever you go, whatever you do, even living with yourself. When you wander in your sleep up to the door of Dracula's evil castle, when you arrive there, your own awakedness will tell you, "Don't go in. Don't do that. Don't hate anyone. Don't think that you know more than what the Truth does, what God does. Don't step inside because if you go too far into the darkness, you won't want to get out."

Do you have just a little bit of a desire right here and now to change things? I didn't say you have to know how to do it because you don't know how to do it. But just having the wish to find a new kind of a life, that would be enough. That is the beginning of giving God Himself the opportunity to hand the cross to you so that it will become your permanent possession. And once you have that cross fully, it will illuminate your whole life and you'll never, ever lose it. Therefore, you'll never, ever lose your life to hostile Dracula-like forces. The cross is true. Ally yourself with that and with nothing else.

Once upon a time there was a school. And let's make this an interesting school. This was a school, a very rare one, for locating lost airplanes. Now if you ever read the news or read books, you will know that every year around the world thousands of airplanes, especially small ones, take off from the airport, go off into the wild blue yonder— *(Laughter)* Shall I sing it? I refuse to sing it— and are never seen again.

This school was founded for the purpose of training men and women to go out and find lost airplanes because there are many reasons why you should, of course. For one thing, there might be clues as to why they got lost and then that information could be used to prevent it from happening again. And so the school started.

Lots of men and women came the first day and the instructor gave them an introduction to the whole class and then the course, in which he explained how some airplanes had been found after being lost for as much as fifty years up in remote mountains. He told about one very startling strange case where an airplane had been found in a city park in the lake right in the middle of the city surrounded by a million people. One airplane lost for a long time had been found right in the middle of the lake in the middle of the city park. It had been around millions of people for years, but it had glided in one stormy night and no one was around and it sunk. Nobody ever thought that it might have been down there, but there it was, down there all these years.

The instructor was a good teacher. Do you know why he was a good teacher? Because he never put up with nonsense from any student. And where you have students, you have human beings. And where you have human beings, you have lazy bums. How many of you were pretty awful students in school? How many of you have learned better since then? That's what we're here for. Maybe you've learned a little bit. So the class went on and the teacher was a firm disciplinarian and he gave them rules to follow.

He said, "Now, you've got to follow these rules because this is what's going to make you a good airplane locator. You can go out any place in the world where they call you. Maybe a government on the other side of the world in Australia or South America, might call you because you're an expert and they want that plane located for lots of reasons. So, ladies and gentlemen, you must obey the rules."

But they were lazy and all they wanted to know was, "How much money am I going to get out of locating it and how much will my name be in the newspaper?" People are that way. "Never mind the work, just tell me how I can get the reward." So he was very, very tough on them, which means he was a right teacher. But they were lazy and he had to discipline some of them. They wouldn't obey the rules.

One day an old pro came to the class who was a friend of the teacher. And this old pro was an old pro at finding lost airplanes around the world. He'd found hundreds of them and so he gave a talk before the class and told them about his experiences, some of the methods he'd used for locating planes. For example, they should know that a plane could be well under the brush and completely covered. You can't see it from the air so you have to go on by foot and so on, all the little tricks of the trade of locating lost airplanes.

The lecture was over and they took a break. The guest speaker was interesting and a lot of the class gathered around him. But many started complaining about the discipline of the teacher. They said, "Aw, he makes it too tough for us. A certain amount of homework is okay, but he makes us work all night long so that we can't go out and have a good time at night. And everybody has to have a good time."

He listened to all their complaints and semi-insults of the teacher. When they were all through, he sat there and eyed them very quietly and said, "You ought to be ashamed of yourselves for what you're doing. Don't you know that that man is the best friend you have because he will not put up with the laziness and the nonsense that you put up with? If you had someone who just wanted to be liked and accepted, he'd let you get away with it. This man won't, so he's your best friend. But I want to tell you something else," the old-timer said, "Try to revise your thinking about these rules. First of all, they're on your side." And he emphasized one point. He said, "Now come on, ladies and gentlemen. Where did you ever get the notion that the rules are your enemy? They're not!"

Let me leap in. Where did you ever get the notion that the spiritual rules are your enemy? The enemy in you calls them an enemy. The simple action of yielding to rightness when you don't want to yield, will make you a skilled locator of lost parts inside of you. That's one of the parallels, isn't it? Finding a lost airplane is like finding our lost self. Now God Himself is one hundred percent tough, a stern disciplinarian with no nonsense. Why don't you join him? If that's the way Reality operates, isn't that the perfect example for you to not put up with what wants to keep you lost?

And here's a little side thought. When you have found yourself, then and only then will you be capable of helping other people to find themselves. Because if you have the experience, you've gone through it. You know that the spiritual rules are the only thing that really loves you.

Have you ever thought about that? Let's do it right now. You want to be loved, don't you? That is not wrong. That is right to want to be loved, but look what you choose as a love—your own hardness and neuroses. Look what you choose to love you. No wonder you're hugged to where you can barely breathe. You ask for Dracula to love you. He will very delightfully fly in the window as a bat and land on your bed and he'll love you. And in the morning you'll know why you feel drained, hopefully.

Follow the thought again. If you want to be loved authentically, there is a way for you to put yourself in that position. And the way you put yourself in that position is to remember that there's only one love. How many do you have? You're chasing around hoping that you can find love inside yourself. Forget it. No human being, no human personality is capable of love.

Now look, you better get your language straightened out, too. Love is not physical affection. Pure love could express itself through physical affection. A true teacher might pat a student on the shoulder as he goes by, something like that. True love is not as you define it, want or expect it to be. The whole problem is that you are defining love according to you.

Will you run out of yourself? Will you walk away from yourself? Will you refuse, as we do in this class, to think that just because you know the word love that you have it? Talking about love, what's that? It's the word. And when you have real love, you won't have to talk about it. It'll be there. There's really only one love, which is Truth, Reality, the only thing that you can connect with that will lift you up toward itself.

Dracula and Wolf Man and the rest of them, when you get attracted to them, drag you down. But here's something very deep to realize. Your present nature, being without love, will pray for hate. Yes! You'll pray for trouble and you'll get them. I once told you it all depends on who you're praying to. If you pray to Dracula and Wolf Man, they'll answer your prayers. They'll come around and they'll attack you. What is wrong with you that you don't understand that? Don't you dare bawl and feel sorry for yourself the next time you get into trouble with anything, anywhere, anyhow. Don't you dare cry out, "Persecution!" You wanted Dracula in your house or he wouldn't have been there. If he's there, it's because you in your unloving nature wanted hatred there, which Dracula represents.

Now you're asking, "Who is going to pray to God in order to get light and goodness and health into my life? Who's going to pray for that? You said that I don't have anything but a Dracula nature inside myself. Where can I find the me who's going to pray to God?" Don't ask that question. That question is always asked in desperation, and desperation is a part of darkness. And you're trying to deceive yourself into thinking that *you* really want God. You can *never* want God. You can only want Dracula. If you understood all this, you would disappear. And the disappearance of you attracts the Spirit of Truth, the Spirit of God. Then that will take possession of you instead of Dracula.

I know your difficulty. You're trying to do with the mind what must be done with the Spirit.

Come to the end of your mind, please. Come to the end of your false intelligence by which you are trying to figure out what I'm telling you. Don't try to figure out in your present low-level way what I'm trying to tell you. Instead, take a broom and sweep your present ways of thinking out of the house, out of your mental house. Take a broom and sweep it out completely. Then you'll understand. You will understand because you won't be there anymore.

See, you want to be the understander. You can never be the understander. When you walk away from yourself, when you sweep yourself out of the way, *you* are not there. Then there is *The Understander,* but it is not you, and you'll understand exactly what that means. When you go, when you disappear, you'll understand perfectly what that disappearance means. Yes, you have a mind and you're using your mind in its proper place, but besides that mind you now have something that you didn't have before, which is the Spirit and you know that that Spirit is not yours. You didn't create it. You did your part of getting rid of your Dracula thoughts and impulses and desires. When Dracula goes, Truth comes.

• • •

The Mystery of Dracula
Part IV

The less life in a person, the more he will try to live off of your life. Dracula and Dracula-type human beings are always hungry for psychological junk food. The process of trying to live off another human being is constant and unseen. Therefore, human beings, being unconscious of this, suffer needlessly. Because if you knew what was happening to you at the hands of other people, it couldn't happen anymore. However, you have a severe problem and responsibility that you don't see. You don't understand that you yourself are a part of the trading process. And we're going to discuss that this morning.

I use the phrase "Dracula-type people," and from now on, when you hear the term Dracula, I want you to always add to it the phrase "Dracula-type men and women." This will enable you to understand that the total evil of Dracula, who represents Satan, is not just in him. It's not down in hell or in the castle in Transylvania. The horrible, weird, sick, hideous evil that Dracula represents is in human beings. Now, where else could it be? It can be invisible, but it occupies human beings. It's not in the door of the castle. It's not in the walls. It's not in the windows. It's not in the chairs. Evil inhabits human beings.

Now at the sound of that statement, human beings of the Dracula-type, which is practically everyone, recoil and don't want to think about that anymore. We're getting a little bit closer to where the Dracula-type could be exposed by the information, and that's the last thing any human being wants to do. He doesn't want to be exposed in his prowling around, and that's a pretty good word. I want you to watch yourself prowling around. I'm talking to you. I'm talking to you about Dracula. I'm talking to you about evil. I'm talking to you about why you suffer, why you're lost. You have done the wrong thing with your inner life. You've done the wrong thing with your spirit. And I want you to know that you are doing the wrong thing anytime you prowl around trying to get anything whatever from any other human being outside of the physical necessities of life.

Please leave spirituality to God Himself instead of thinking that you can avoid God, Truth, Reality and trick other people and drain them and steal from them and use them and exploit them in order to get what you need. You will get what you think you need, what you've deluded yourself into thinking you need, and you will always be hungry. Dracula and Dracula-types are always famished. They must always have more. That is why they're always on the prowl and in ways unimaginable, and when you first see the whole story of what I'm talking about, you'll be stunned, shocked and astonished that you yourself—yes, you—have been a very, very close part of the Dracula story.

That is a good thing for you to see. Don't avoid it any more. Be willing to understand what you're hearing here right now. It's the only chance you have for salvation from yourself. You think you can get deliverance, ease, comfort, strength from someone else? You've never done it. Oh, how much of your life have you wasted trying to find something in a human being that you can only get from God? But you see, Dracula-types don't want God. They want to be their own God. And anything that suggests that you have to give up your pride, your vanity and your egotism in exchange for what is true and virtuous and good, any suggestion of that is fearfully pushed away.

Speaking of the word fear, let's look at that in connection with vampirism, human vampirism. Human beings give fear and are given fear in return, right? You know personally, if you will examine yourself now while I'm talking, what an overwhelming flood of emotion fear is in your life. It was there this morning, for example. But did you see it? That's what we're talking about. Did you have the anti-Dracula light enough this morning as you were getting ready to come here to look and see how afraid you are? Your nature as it presently is has no choice but to be fearful.

Now, I said that Dracula-types feed off of other people. Having no life of their own, they must prowl around, and I'll give you specific examples of it in a little bit. They're looking for something to get, hopeful that this time it's going to be the right nutrition that's going to give them life. It's an impossible task and you might as well stop it right now.

You *can* stop it right now without fully understanding it, so don't use the evasion that you don't know what I'm talking about. Something in you knows exactly what I'm talking about. As a matter of fact there are two things inside of you that know exactly what I'm saying. The wrong part of you knows and it hates it, and the right part of you knows it and wants to encourage you to kick out the wrong part. Yes, underneath it all, as much as you try to block it out, it will seep through. You know that I'm giving you the proper plan of salvation for your own individual soul. You know that.

All right. Arousing fear, human vampires, who live in fear, can only give what they are, what they have. And you pass fear on to everyone else by your expression, by your manner, by your voice, by your words, by what you do. And then, when they get frightened in return, which keeps the whole world terrified, that becomes your food. You need more of what you are, whether it's good or evil. In this case, it's evil.

In this case, you've got to have more fear. You've got to look around and tell people the bad things that are happening to you and how you couldn't help getting into that problem because other people did it to you. Someone else is always at fault, of course. And you're shaking and you're trembling and you're having the worst time of your life. And you were actually hoping that the response from the world, from individuals, will also be more fear because that's all you have and that's all you know about. Therefore, you are fiercely hungry for more of that. You fear to run out of fear because if you didn't have it, who would you be? You could no longer be Dracula which you now delight in being. You can no longer be a vampire who drains other people, who takes from them. If you were not a taker, a drainer, who would you be? "I don't know who I'd be!" Find out.

You're going to have to go that far. You're going to have to do what I said, to understand thoroughly, completely, altogether that all you want is what you now have. You're going to have to want something else. I'll tell you a point that's ten million miles high. Your fear of non-existence for giving up your false life is false. Any fear you have of not existing after you follow the spiritual rules, that fear is false. I'm telling you that, and again you now have no reason to evade and postpone and refuse to give up your life of fear. Your fear of giving up fear is a part of you, therefore, a part of something that's worthless, useless. Drop it now. God will catch you. God will take you because you have finally given him the chance to do that.

Who catches you now? Don't you run from

one anxiety to the next? As much as you talk to your spouse, as much as you talk to yourself, it never, never goes away. The attacks you make upon other people and the attacks of other people on you are constant. Nothing ever changes. And I tell you that, unless you follow to the very end of what you're hearing right now, nothing will change and you'll have no real future at all, no *real* future. Your future will be you. *Your future will be your present nature.*

Can you think of anything worse than you continuing to be the kind of a human being you actually are inside? Not that phony who out-wardly appears to be so happy and cheerful. Knock it off, for heaven's sake. Knock it off, for your sake! Don't you want to be a decent per-son? When you talk to or you're with other people, don't you want to be someone who does not pass on anxiety as you are now doing? You see, *that* is what morality is. Morality is spirituality pos-sessed by you *after* you have dispossessed your own evil.

Here's a special point on Dracula attacks, which should explain many things to you. A Dracula-type human being attacks others. And when he feels especially hungry, which is really all the time, he tries to attack God, good, decency, rightness, truth, virtue. There's a very special false destructive reward for a Dracula-type, for a human being, when he attacks authentic good-ness, which he senses and which he recognizes.

For example, each one of you hearing this talk senses quite clearly inside yourself that what you're hearing is good, virtuous, spiritual. You know that. There's no question about it. So an *eviler*—that's a word originated here to cover all wicked, sick human beings and is a good general word to remember—an *eviler* attacks goodness. The slightest appearance of something that comes from God is picked up by Satanic radar and is immediately attacked because it doesn't want it to spread any further. Its own kingdom of darkness feels threatened so it wants to stop it.

But now here's the interesting point. This is fascinating spiritual psychology. God doesn't fight Satan. You understand that it's only in a figure of speech we say that, to make things clearer. But why should God fight Satan when He has already won? The victory is complete right now and you can join it right now if you want. When a Satanic force, a hostile group or individual attacks a source of Truth, a good place, *God, Truth and God's representatives never fight back.*

Remember that when Satan, Dracula, attacks someone, he does it *wanting* them to fight back. How? By them being afraid, right? That's an opposition. He wants you to be afraid or say, "I'm not afraid of you," or some other lie. They love a fight-back. But what happens when—and this is a very rare case because there's so little Truth in this world to oppose evil—Satan attacks Truth and

Truth doesn't fight back? Oh, what is Dracula going to do? He attacks in order to get food, but the attack doesn't come back so he doesn't get food.

You see, he can get any gullible human being on earth he wants to feed him by being drained and being in fear and so on. Ah, but I told you, God never loses. And in his own evil, sick way, Satan never loses. He always has a reserve. Evil attacks goodness. Goodness remains poised and calm, totally strong and with complete understanding and does not fight back.

Then, how is Dracula going to get fed when there's no reaction? Ah, it's simple. Remember, I'm talking about Dracula-like human beings. He generates his own hatred of God for not fighting him, and *that's* his fight. And add to that the fact that the battle is always inside the evil person. It can't be inside a good person.

So when Satan attacks God, when an evil person attacks an authentically good person—who is very rare as I said before—when there is no fight back, there is a specially fierce rage and violent hatred because that is a recognition by Satan that God is good. The one thing that Satan can't stand is the *goodness of God*.

Do you see why Satan, Dracula feels fed when you fight back? Your fighting back is evil and he knows you're evil and therefore his cunning evil can win over your stupid evil. He loves that and his attack is continuous. But when God, when

Christ, when the cross doesn't fight back—in order to not lose his dinner—he becomes fearfully enraged at the simple fact that God is God and doesn't need to fight back. And that exposure of Satan's own actual powerlessness throws him into an insane rage, and you can't believe what that human being will do in his total insanity and hatred of God and goodness. He'll destroy the whole world if he can.

I'm telling you right now and you have to make some connections. The rage that Dracula feels at the existence of God is the basic cause of all human problems, from the war inviting and involving the whole world, to the little cruel sniping of human beings at each other in the family.

Transfer your allegiance right now from what you are now to something else that you have sensed is right. This is the start. I want to make quite sure you understand. Don't think you can go out of here and do it on your own. You'll be deceived again and you'll go right back to where you started, not knowing what happened to you.

If you want to learn to speak French or play the violin, you don't go to one lesson. You have to go back and back to it until you finally learn it. It's the same with this. You must be at a place where the French language or the violin playing are taught in order to understand it. You have to attend your spiritual lessons in order to go on from where you are. I tell you that because you, in your present state of ignorance and vanity, do not know the vast and persistent trickery and deceit of Dracula, who is Satan, who is everything that wants to destroy you.

Think of the word *draining*. That's what Dracula is all about, taking life from someone else. He has none of his own so he must prey on other people. And so he goes after them and drains their life in any way he can. Let's find a few examples.

I talked to you about Dracula and his types. Let's right now, you adding your own thoughts to this, look at some Dracula draining types. How about the complainer? Did you ever stop to connect that with Dracula? No, you haven't. Now you will. Now you'll understand that we have to bring this business of vampires, of evil right down, very close and very personal.

Can you think of people right now as I'm talking who drain you? How do they do it? Through their demands. A demander is a drainer through their intimidation of you, through constantly harassing you in some way or another, asking endless, stupid questions or writing you notes or making telephone calls. You understand how we must indeed bring this right down to daily life.

See, wherever there's contact between any two people, there's an exchange of energy. It goes from the stronger to the weaker. This is a law, and in itself this law can be helpful to you if you understand it, not helpful if you don't understand it. Right now, energy is going down-hill in this room. That is, it's coming from the higher through the source of Truth and being given to you right now. That's one operation of the law, the strength going down from the higher to the weaker. Now all human beings are weak, so what do they do? They drain each other in an exchange of energy.

As an exercise, make a list, as long a list as you want, and I want you do this. This is your practical work. You can't just sit back and listen and think you understand it. You won't but you'll kid yourself into thinking you know everything that the talk was all about. You don't know how to apply it to your practical life. Make a list. And this list will keep going for as long as you want it to, but for at least a week; a year would be much better.

Put up at the top of the list: *How I Am Drained.* And you will number them: One, a very short sentence. Two, the second short sentence. Third, next. Fourth, next. That person you met at the supermarket and you really didn't want to talk to him, did you? Who was it? A neighbor, friend, someone you work with, but he saw you first and you weren't able to wheel your cart out of the way fast enough. *(Laughter)* I'll give you a hint. Always keep your grocery basket light so that you can move it fast when necessary. *(Laughter)* Put him on your list.

How about the telephoner? The person who

puts you in a spot is a good one, and that connects with the person who asks you a lot of
foolish, useless questions. Do you know why they
ask you questions? Obviously it's not because
they want the answers, but because they want to
blab. The blabber.

And, by the way, you better turn the page
over on the other side and keep another list: *How
I Drain Myself.* There's both sides to it, you
know. How many of you talk to yourself? You
know you do. You mutter to yourself. How many
of you give yourself the greatest solutions in
the world to your problems? How many of you
know exactly how to save the world? And the
next day it's gone and there's something else in
its place. Being drained by others and draining
yourself, get them both on the list.

And these are to be very specific examples.
And your list, eventually, shouldn't be any shorter
than the time you have to put into it. Maybe you'll
have a hundred or more. And then you're to go
over it. Never write anything down without ex-
amining it later on because the next time or
second or third or tenth time, you'll see something you didn't see before. You know that's a
rule, too, where review and examination give you
more than the first time you put it down on a
piece of paper.

How are you going to stop yourself from
draining others, from being the cause of trouble
to them? Why do you love being a source of

trouble to others? Now don't deny it! Your very nature is a source of trouble.

Shall I describe your nature so you'll understand what I'm talking about? It's weakness. Tell me one thing you have besides mental weakness, emotional-wild weakness, life weakness? You don't have any strength at all. You just have a pack of memories and ideas about strength. You have your phony, lying quotations ready. You've got your quick answers. In other words, you've got your self-destruction built-in solidly to protect yourself against the very idea that you are weak. Why don't you admit it right now? I know it's going to put you through a crisis and it's about time. You've refused the crisis of seeing that you're weak and lost.

Enter it now. And as your weakness falls away, strength, authentic strength, which is always spiritual, never mental, never man-made, never created by a sick society, but real strength will come to you. But you have to face it, you have to bravely go into it.

Remember the word *eviler* again and then I'm going to go on to a story, but I want to tell you that the word *eviler* is so essential for you to apply to yourself and to everyone else. Who do you know who is a good man? Who do you know who's good? You don't know anyone at all. Tell me. Oh, come on. You think they're good because you think you're good, and you project your own false goodness and say they're good too, and now you have two Dracula-types draining each other. Knock it off.

Once upon a time there was a good emperor of a big country. And this emperor had a lot of foolish subjects. And they would wander around to the edge of the kingdom after being warned not to do it. And finally, a large group of them became lost on the outskirts of the kingdom in the wilderness. By the way, you understand being lost is symbolic of your condition. Are you lost or found? Which are you? If you have hatred in you, you're lost. Do you have anger in you? You're lost. Do you have confusion in you? You're lost. If you have pretense in you, you are lost. If you think you're found, you are lost.

The kindly, compassionate emperor decided to send a messenger to these foolish people who refused to listen to the warnings of the good King, which means God in this story. But they refused to listen. They knew better. They didn't come back to the King for continued lessons week after week and year after year in order to get rid of the mess that they had been living in. They decided to think on their own and go on their own, and so now they're weeping, crying, hostile little children out in the dark places.

The emperor decided to send a messenger to them with a map, a map that would tell them how to get back. He would give them the map, they could see it and if they weren't too far gone to hear and see and understand the map, if they weren't too far gone, those individuals could come back.

Those who are too far gone would not want to come back because now they take their delight in the kingdom of hell, in the kingdom of darkness, while lying about it and saying that it's a good place to be. How could it ever be a good thing to be lost, to be a hateful, hostile, lying, hypocritical human being, either religious or non-religious? How can it be good? I'll tell you, total insanity means that the individual has convinced himself that he is all right and everyone else is all wrong.

The messenger took the map and started down the road. He had a long journey reaching them because these people had gone earlier on a long wandering journey themselves. He had the map in his pocket and he was a good representative of the good king. He knew that nothing could stop him from delivering this message because he had done it many times before. But I want to tell you what happened. And please see that I'm talking about Truth and what happens to Truth when it is presented to a sick, dark world. You'll see it. You'll understand it under the surface of your mind.

At a certain place the messenger had to pass down a long narrow road. And on both sides of this road were tall thick trees. There was no way the messenger could leave the road between the trees because they were so thick. He started down the road and he looked up and what he saw was something that you see, but now scares you. And by the end of this talk, you will have all you need to no longer be afraid of what you see for the first time. It's there to see but you haven't seen it yet because you're too afraid to see it and understand it. What he saw perched at the top of the trees were hundreds of vicious vampire bats with red eyes glowing with hatred and sharp beaks and claws. They were staring down at the messenger who had the map. They knew he had the map. They can tell. Dracula-types, I told you before, can tell when Truth comes along in this world and tries to help the few wanderers out of the million who want to be saved.

I'd better leave the story for just a minute to ask you, do you want to be saved? Or are you so permanently in love with yourself that you have no intention of ever coming back to where you really belong? Since when do you belong in a place, an inner place, where there's nothing but concealed lies and confusion inside of you? It doesn't make any sense, does it? Does it make any sense at all to be a miserable, sick, lying human being? It doesn't make any sense at all, but you think it does. Many people think that it does and so they cling to that.

The messenger started down this narrow road and then the vulture-like bats began their work. They swooped down, dozens at a time. You see, vultures hang out together. No vampire bat or vulture can ever live alone psychologically. He must surround himself with bats who are just as sick and evil and as vicious as he is. Bats flock together. They swooped down and attacked him viciously, dozens at a time, hundreds at a time. They knocked him down. Then that flock went away, which gave the messenger time to get up and make sure the map was still in his pocket, which it was every time. He wasn't going to lose that map.

And there's no way you can ever take the map away from a human being who has once accepted it from God, from the Emperor. No way. *Once you accept it personally from the High Source, the very accepting of it means that you know the only power is God.* And no matter how much the vicious vampires attack you along the way, *it's no contest.* It makes no difference how badly you're attacked.

Now, I have to tell you all something. You're not anywhere yet near this position where you are in this narrow road with the vicious bats swooping down on you. You haven't declared yourself authentically and publicly for God yet. You see, you're still hiding out. You want someone else to take the chances and to be daring. You want someone else to be the spokesman.

You must be a messenger, but you must let God tell you how to do that. Because there's a woman over there and there's a man over there and there's a person who's twenty years old over there, a man who's sixty years old over there, and God uses everyone in his own way. And once you take the map, you will be told individually how you should bring it to other people. So don't think you must imitate anyone else in the way they do it. Isn't that nice to know? God knows how you should do it and He will tell you once you accept it.

The map stayed firmly in the messenger's pocket and he went on and on. And do you remember I said to you that this road represents your life here. You don't know how insanely vicious and hideous and totally destructive and maniacal this world is. The world really, in fact, is made up of nothing but vicious vampire bats who want to destroy the messengers if they can. You can't destroy the messenger, by the way. You can knock him down. You can slander him.

And so, this happened to the messenger on the road we're talking about, and every time he was knocked down, he got up and went on and on and on. And the farther he went, the more enraged the vampires became and the more ferocious became their attack. He went on and on and finally he got to the end of that particular journey. He went to where the dark land was, where all the lost subjects of the king were bewailing their lot, hard and bitter that they were suffering so much, never knowing that they had made that choice for themselves. And so do you. If you're suffering, you've chosen it, and don't you be a weak little coward who says you didn't. Wherever you are right now is what you have chosen for yourself, and if you will admit that, God can give you the map and help you. If you lie about it, nothing can be done for you. Good-bye.

The messenger showed the map to all the thousands of people lost out there, and out of the thousands, only one or two or three wanted to take it and come back home. You have to be one of those. Lose your desire to be a vampire and a drainer, because you're either one of those bats on top of the tree or you're a messenger of God. One of the two.

And I will add one more little point and then we'll have to stop. Here's a second exercise. You will now see how you are a visual vampire. You glare and you stare and you're trying to drain other people and trying to make people afraid of you staring and glaring at them. Don't do that anymore.

I want to leave this as the final thought to you and you use it as your guide and your inspiration. Think about it. I tell you, the stars are not too high to reach. ***The stars are not too high to reach.***

• • •

The Mystery of Dracula

Part V

I will read aloud and answer a few questions as follows.

Question: *What is the meaning behind getting bitten by Dracula or by one of his vampires? I can sense its significance but it is not clear.*

The first thing to remember about being bitten by a human vampire is that you were a willing victim. There was something in you that thought that putting yourself under the sick power of another human being would do something for you. What? Take away your insecurity? Why do you ever submit your life to anyone else for anything? There's no point in it. Nothing good can come from it. But because you're weak, you attribute strength to another person and think they can help you.

Never, never submit yourself to the thoughts, to the ideas of any human being because God says there is something higher than that. If you want to submit yourself, why don't you submit yourself to the Truth that you sense exists, but which you don't have the intelligence or the humility to just drop your pride and let God tell you what you are all about. You don't know what you are all about and no other human being is ever going to be able to tell you. When he bites you, he's going to drain you instead of give you something.

See, it's so odd that nobody ever learns. You never learn! Now, don't you go out of here and not learn! Again, it's time you stopped! This is it, I'm telling you. For all of you listening to this, *this is it for you.* I told you earlier about that decision. Don't fall in love and stay in love with delusion and self-deception. You'd better start the study of self-deception right now and never, never say you've completed the course. Then you'll never allow any other human being to bite you with a promise that he's going to give you something, that smooth-talking Dracula or that female vampire.

God has provided a way for you to live from Him and not from any human being. And only that will make you safe in this world of human beings who are all Draculas in disguise. And it's about time you had the intelligence to say, "I'm going to investigate that until I see the truth of it."

Question: *I'm glad that other people can't read my mind because I have so many bad thoughts about sex, about revenge and other awful things that I don't want anyone to know about. What do I need?*

Just know that your bad thoughts are destroying you. What else do you need? No, you don't know that yet. You like thoughts of revenge, vampire thoughts, thinking they're giving you life when they're really draining you. Look, if a bunch of bats flew into your backyard at night and stole the fruit or whatever bats eat, wouldn't you want to stop them? Maybe you have a light on the back porch and you've got to stand by that light switch all the time, and when you turn on that light the bats that have come flying down into your fruit orchard are going to fly away. The bats are draining your life. The fruit represents your life that's being drained because you are asleep in your bed instead of by that light switch.

Here you'll learn what the light is. You'll learn that the light is stronger than the bats and all the Draculas that invade your life. But you have to be by the switch. It has to be on all the time. You can't be careless and let it go off. You, by God's power, have to keep the light switch on all the time.

Oh! You'll be absolutely amazed at how the bats will fly out of your life and not bother you anymore. If you're not going to give them something, they're not going to hang around anymore. They're going to flutter off to find the next gullible victim that they can drain.

When you cease being drained, you will automatically and naturally feel a new flow of strength, simply because when that new strength comes to you, it stays with you instead of being taken away by a thief. And you'll feel it. And you won't be ableto explain it to anyone, maybe, but you will feel it because you are living it.

Question: *While I want to find someone higher and nicer, I'm really not sure what I'm supposed to do. Please give me specific ideas to act upon.*

I was thinking of an example of that. Let's take out a part of a Dracula movie scene, one scene that is very likely to be in the *Dracula* movie. You'll recognize it. Here's the woman, the heroine, a young pretty girl, and she's standing at the bottom of the steps of the castle and she's terrified and you can see it in her eyes. She's standing at the bottom of the steps looking up, one hand on the railing. She knows she has to go up there, but she doesn't know what's up there. Is Dracula hiding in the shadows at the top of the room? Are the bats going to swoop down on her? She knows she has to go up: one foot on the first step, the other foot on the floor, her hand on the railing, standing up scared. I've described your life.

You know what you can do and what you must do and what we'll teach you to do. Now come on, that's fear. She's terrified. I'll tell you, you're that woman, you're that man. You're afraid of everything. You are, you're afraid of everything. You're terrified of yourself. You don't know who's in there. You don't understand that alien, that stranger. You're absolutely terrified all day long over yourself, to say nothing of other people.

I'll tell you what to do, we'll teach you here. You take one step up and then you take another step up, and then you take another step up and your hand will go alongside you on the railing. And you'll just keep walking until you get to the top of the stairs and you'll see that there's nothing there. Dracula is at the bottom of the steps!

He's the woman! The man! The fearful person! But you have to find that out. You don't believe it now. You've never done it. You have to do it. Dracula isn't up there. He's with you. He's inside you.

Question, when you're terrified, where's the terror? In the lamppost down the street? In the piece of toast in the toaster? The terror is in you. How are you going to get rid of it? We'll show you how to call the bluff on Dracula, on that person who intimidates you, who you know is really demented. How many know a demented person? You know them. All bats are demented and all demented people are bats. We'll show you how to take one step at a time while being as afraid as you are. Did you ever hear anything greater than that?

You say, "How can I get rid of fear?" We tell you, don't get rid of fear. Work in spite of fear, one step at a time. I guarantee you that at the top of the steps, there are no terrors, only the light. But you have to make the journey. You have to do the climbing.

Question: *I can feel surrounding dangers, but I can't understand them. Please supply what we must do to be safe and to know we are safe.*

I was reading a story about sailing ships of a couple of hundred years ago. And do you know what they did to be safe? They did what you have to do. Safety, to them, represented staying close to shore where there's the harbor, the harbors and

139

the lights. Here are all these storms of life and you insist on sailing out on the raging seas when you don't have to. Again, we'll teach you how to stay close to shore where the harbor is.

Now you're all involved in storms, aren't you? All of you nod your head either mentally or physically. You are all involved in life's storms and you're afraid you're going to sink, aren't you? You are so terrified of the storm. The next storm that you have—which is any minute now, by the way—you will let it drive you closer to shore instead of further out into that raging sea. This can and must be done. You've simply made the wrong choice. You didn't know that you have within you the free will and the choice to turn toward the safe harbor instead of going further out to sea where there's nothing but terror. Turn toward shore and I will tell you that the heavenly harbor is there waiting for you. All you have to do is turn and go toward it. And one day you will know the difference between choosing to let the storm carry you out to sea or back to harbor. Do you want the harbor? It is there waiting for you.

Now, whatever you've heard this morning, you take it and absorb it and never, never let anything in your life be more important—no person, no object, no pleasure, no pursuit. This is the most important thing in your life. This is the *only* thing important in your life. And one day you will reach the harbor.

• • •

Chapter 5
He That Hath Ears to Hear, Let Him Hear

Christ gave a statement of astonishing insight, as all true spiritual statements are astonishing and marvelous. That statement went as follows:

"Let he that hath ears to hear, let him hear."

Now, of course, He was not talking about hearing the winds in the hills of Galilee or the sounds of merchants in the market place. As always, He was talking about something above this world. He understood thoroughly that world above this earthly sphere that we live on.

I want you to begin to understand your need to develop spiritual hearing. It will come to you, for example, as you follow the principles that you have just heard. As you listen and want to hear, you will.

That hearing obviously has to be personally experienced by you. When it finally comes, there is no question at all in your mind that you are hearing a message from another world.

Listen to this: you know finally that you are no longer talking to yourself when you have become silent in your mind and in your emotions. *In that silence, God is able to speak to you and you will recognize it.*

Your new hearing is totally unlike anything else. It is immediately recognized when it really happens to you. When it happens, that is the same thing as you changing from a mere human living from thoughts, ambitions and anxieties.

Your nature starts to change so that while you still have a mind, emotions and a physical self, there is a voice giving you instructions about how to get out of the dark cave. This voice that you are hearing is operating on and through your mind, feelings, body, voice, reactions.

Feeling is the same as hearing. And hearing changes what you do with your whole composite nature, self.

You are following the orders of this spiritual voice of God. To your great interest and delight, you find that you don't want to go down to visit your friend's house anymore, to where you were going to have drinks and chatter about non-sensical, trivial things.

You are interested to find out that without making any plans or thinking about it, without conflict, all of a sudden it comes to be eight o'clock and you don't want to go to your friend's house and drink and do whatever foolish things you used to do.

You want to stay home and be with and increasingly enjoy this new nature that is hearing this voice. Oh, you get so eager to hear more. You're not going to hear it down with those beer glasses clicking. You're not going to hear it down there with all those loud voices and you know it.

See what has happened—you have made your choice just to hear. Making that choice, you did hear. And what you heard the voice saying was, "Stay home and let Me talk to you instead of those sick friends, the whole sick world." And it was the easiest choice of your life, right?

What is more pleasurable than to not be under the dragging compulsion of getting in the car, going down there again and putting on the false face as you went in the door. And it's your turn to buy the drink, your turn to lead in the foolishness maybe. Oh what a pleasure to cut off the drain of your whole life.

Nothing is more pleasurable than to be in a position of knowing what Christ was talking about when He said that. You know that you can listen any time you want, twenty-four hours a day. Yes, even while you are asleep. God doesn't sleep. He is always ready to talk to you, twenty-four hours of the day.

You will get such a wish to always be listening. If you begin to catch a chattering mind or you become attracted for the moment to the noisy mob out there, you'll want nothing more than to stay home all the time. The time will come when you'll be able to catch yourself in time.

Being *at home* means living with yourself, with this true nature, which is always receptive, always listening for the little insight, the little warning, the little advice. Then you don't have to think your life as you used to.

143

It drives you crazy to think your own life making decisions, doesn't it? You will not have to do that anymore.

All decisions about how to live a true and truly happy life have already been made. They have been made since Eternity.

They have always been there, but we have been somewhere else. We've been down to our so-called friend's house, wasting our lives.

Stay home and listen. *And you **will** hear.*

• • •

Chapter 6

Freedom from Harmful Voices

YOUR NEW WORLD OF MENTAL PEACE

Tired of mental torment? Good. This publication will reveal two immense facts. It will explain how you are unknowingly victimized by harmful forces. And it will show you how to be free of mental pain forever. True happiness results.

Whether a person is aware of it or not, he is assaulted constantly by misleading and hostile voices within the mind. They speak both through you and to you. Everyone is their target, but because of their extreme cunning, few people ever detect and dismiss them. So the only problem is a lack of information about these foreign voices. The curing facts are as close as your desire for them.

It is extremely important for you to remember the following truth: these hurtful voices are *not you,* and they do not belong to you, but merely speak through your psychic system. Don't take them as being your own voices, any more than you take radio voices as being your own. They simply *use* unaware human beings. Your true nature has nothing to do with them. When finally dismissing these sinister speakers you make room for spiritual health and true life.

It is helpful to give these harmful voices several different names, though they all describe the same enemy. So think also of them as being

145

evil suggestions, hateful spirits, deceitful whisper-ings, mental demons, lying thoughts, indecent in-vaders, fiendish tormentors, cunning deceivers.

The voices either remain inside your mind as silent thoughts and beliefs and attitudes, or can actually speak out by using vocal cords. This chapter concentrates on studying and exposing silent speech.

As you read, notice one result in particular. You will find yourself nodding in agreement at the perfectly accurate descriptions of the voices. *See how much is known about them.* You may recognize some that have tormented you since childhood.

Write down the numbers of those you recog-nize from the past. Review them. This increases wisdom for detecting those still hiding from you.

Dismissal of the dark makes room for the light. True voices will definitely appear to guide you toward lasting security. These higher voices are sane, compassionate, practical—and beautiful.

It is your *recognition* of the hurtful voices that breaks their grip and drives them away. So proceed to the next section, where your recog-nition becomes your power for their dismissal.

HARMFUL VOICES EXPOSED

1. Skilled in imitation, they mimic the scolding voices of your parents, reviving your past fears and shames.

2. To prevent you from finding your own true life they burden you with false responsibilities toward others.

3. At bedtime, recognize the chattering voices that try to rob you of restful sleep.

4. They stir up rage in citizens by reminding them of the weakness and stupidity of people in power.

5. One talkative gang exploits a man's fear of revenge from others, but it can be chased away by decent voices.

6. They exist to harm you only with your unconscious cooperation, so withdraw your cooperation at once.

REMEMBER THIS REVELATION

7. If you ever hear anyone sneering in disbelief at the existence of hateful voices *you are hearing a sneering, hateful voice.*

8. Whispering that retreat from life will keep you safe, they don't tell you that retreat protects and preserves only danger.

9. Few people see how they are tricked into feeling guilty over things they should not think about at all.

10. If they detect the smallest weakness in anyone they will pounce upon him with all the fury of a crazed tiger.

11. They supply a desperate man with dozens of

    stupid solutions, hoping he will frantically take at least one of them.

12. Truth has *already won* the battle against these sinister speakers, which becomes your victory as you join Truth.

SEX TALK

13. When a man sees a desirable woman, a voice torments him by laughing that he will never have sex with her.

14. They delight in ganging up on a victim, all shouting at once to cause intense pain and confusion.

15. Hoping to weaken your spirit, they join with imagination to flash mental scenes of personal and social disasters.

16. Don't be intimidated by those familiar voices which pounce and accuse whenever you make a mistake.

17. They show contempt for weakness and indecision in someone, which they take as an invitation to attack and hurt.

18. Exorcism, the expelling of evil spirit-voices, succeeds when the possessed person yields only to higher powers.

EXPOSE THIS VOICE

19. Hear and recognize the false voice that laughs with contempt toward you when you are rejected by someone.

20. A favorite torment is to force pointless repetitions through the mind, such as the words of a popular song.

21. One voice nags a man to travel, to escape somewhere, when the real need is for an inner journey toward the light.

22. They instruct people to admire public heroes, knowing that these false heroes will lead them into the swamp.

23. Some people hear the scream that they are too far gone for self-rescue, which is simply a lying scream.

24. Healthy voices have no fear of unwell voices, but unwell voices fear and flee before healthy voices.

FALSE FRIENDS

25. They assure you that your friends would not do that to you, and when you believe it your friends do that to you.

26. One evil voice assures someone that God himself supports a certain wrong belief, thus betraying the believer.

27. Nothing is too low for them, for example, they speak lewd and crude words and then try to shame you for having them.

28. A lunatic voice gives itself away by suddenly turning hostile when you question its sanity.

29. They close a man's eyes to light and then call it evidence of the nonexistence of light.

30. The source of any true and helpful voice is God, Truth, Reality, which is All-Powerful all the time.

A WHISPERED ATTACK

31. A devilish voice causes a woman severe agony by whispering that her man might leave her.

32. Hoping you will try to buy a friendship, they supply a dozen lies to make it look like a good bargain.

33. When you see and hear defeated people during your day the voices demand that you also feel like a loser.

34. A man who can't even govern his own life is told he qualifies to govern others in public office, causing public chaos.

35. When a man is wrong they command him to insist that he is right, which keeps the man a tragic slave.

36. To increase your life-power, realize that a harmful voice *can never ever really make sense.*

A STARTLING FACT

37. The world is not ruled by people or laws or money but by destructive voices unheard by the masses on earth.

38. One voice tries to waste your life by urging you to join others who waste their lives in the foolish and the trivial.

39. Reject a mental voice that suddenly takes you over to shriek angrily at someone who has offended you.

40. Millions pay a heavy price to a voice that appeals to vanity by telling people that they are not appreciated as much as they are worth.

41. One voice wants you to feel persecuted by life, but it is the ghastly voice itself that persecutes and hurts.

42. Fear of people in authority falls away as you replace unnatural suggestions with natural voices.

START YOUR DAY RIGHT

43. Don't fall under the voice that starts early in the morning to predict a dull and defeated day for you.

44. You are never really betrayed by other people but only by voices that urge you to trust deceitful people.

45. Recognize a voice that exploits your insecurity, such as one that insists that you must be popular with other people.

46. When a voice says you are the victim of harmful gossip, simply know that it has nothing to do with your true self.

47. What is called bad luck is simply the result of not knowing about and chasing out the malicious mental voices.

48. Quarrels and other problems at home will decrease as you see the voices as constant troublemakers.

PROBLEMS WITH FINANCES

49. Financial confusions arise from inner confusions, which can be cured with clear, spiritual thinking.

50. Understanding the voices reveals the actual motives of people, which protects you from their trickery.

51. Some demon voices do their best work on shallow minds that cannot see that *religious words* are not *spiritual virtues*.

52. The faint voice urging you to live your own free life is trying to make itself heard above the mob voices.

53. Say *NO* firmly to the voice that urges you to give things to other people just to please or disarm them.

54. When they declare that they know what is best for you, look what their past advice has done against you.

REJECT THIS JEERING VOICE

55. One voice comments on the television news, taunting you on your helplessness before frightening events.

56. They urge you to revolt against your present unhappy life, then lead you into a worse state than before.

57. One trick to make you feel bad is to compare your life with other people, making you feel jealous and cheated.

58. Incredibly, they deceive millions with false religious peace by softly muttering nonsensical religious phrases.

59. They insist they have absolute power over you, which you should realize is an absolute lie.

60. You can listen to true voices or to false voices, and since everything depends upon your choice, select the true.

UNDERSTAND INDECISION

61. Painful indecision and mind-changing is simply one wrong voice demanding to be heard, followed by the next and the next.

62. One voice drains a person's energy by forcing him to speak sympathetic words he does not mean.

63. Refuse the voice that tempts you to accuse before you think, for that releases self-healing and self-harmony.

64. To chain his victim to the past, and prevent his freedom in the present moment, one voice praises the holding of grudges.

65. When you are all by yourself they suddenly blurt out aloud with all sorts of repressed and strange thoughts.

66. Demon voices try to use dreams to terrify, but the true nature has total power to maintain peace and rest.

WHEN PEOPLE INTERFERE

67. Don't listen to a resentful voice when other people interfere with your life, but listen to a voice that reveals solutions.

68. Knowing that knowledge is power and confidence in daily affairs, they persuade people to substitute bluff and fakery.

69. No human system for social improvement will ever work as long as people refuse to investigate and remove false voices.

70. Self-rewarding judgment appears by ceasing to surrender the mind to the judgment of the false voices.

71. They often use a man's voice when he speaks aloud, but they hope he does not hear how weak or weird he sounds.

72. The true power needed for banishing harmful forces is available at all times to those who ask for it.

LIVE YOUR OWN LIFE

73. No voice has a life of its own, which is why it fiercely resists your attempt to stop it from using your life.

74. They promise to supply you with the winning words in a forthcoming situation, then give you foolish blurts.

75. To prevent detection of their disguised evil they solemnly warn you against disguised evil.

76. They encourage harmful hysteria by telling people that hysterical behavior will attract attention and sympathy.

77. Notice the ways they suddenly take someone over, as with impulsive shouts or groans or squeals.

78. A depressed voice will try to make your feelings follow it down into sadness and defeat, but alertness prevents this.

A COMMON AND CRUEL VOICE

79. One taunting voice attacks a man with sarcastic remarks about the man's failures in his career and moneymaking.

80. They stir up memories of unpleasant events in an attempt to distract and discourage a spiritual seeker.

81. To create inner conflict they demand obedience to a certain moral or religious code, then tell you to hate it.

82. A criminal thought-voice torments by telling people that their hidden sins will be exposed and punished.

83. Evil voices belong to a large self-protecting club in which all will attack when one of their own is rebuked by Truth.

84. If you are ever tempted to feel friendly toward a softly deceiving voice, remember that your injury is *its very reason for living.*

155

HOW THEY ACCUSE

85. Insisting that you are too stupid to learn, they add torment by running mental movies through your mind of past follies.

86. Any voice that justifies hatred and tries to explain it away is dedicated to causing misery and destruction everywhere.

87. They block self-rescue by supplying a man with lying arguments for convincing himself that he is already rescued.

88. One voice torments by regretfully talking about missed opportunities in the past for financial or sexual conquest.

89. They do not want you to catch them in their evil speech and will use every lie and threat to prevent their exposure.

90. Simply try to see for yourself where wrong thought-voices have promised you a gain but left you with a loss.

THE VOICE OF BETRAYAL

91. They are loud in praising quick thrills, such as angry replies, hoping you will listen, obey and pay in suffering.

92. One speaker says it is safe to reveal your personal secrets to others, then laughs and leaves you to their treachery.

93. Many voices have learned to sing like nightingales, but once the victim comes close they swoop down like vultures.

94. They are fiercely eager to supply reasons why you should attack anyone who tells you about the higher life.

95. A cunningly dangerous voice is one that urges a man to take revenge, then supplies him with evil justifications.

96. Remember that thought-voices are utterly wild, having no self-control, but are conquered by your higher spirit.

AVOID THIS TRAP

97. They convince you that you need a certain person in your life, then trap you with an unpleasant person.

98. One voice promises that you will not repeat a mistake, then slyly leads you into making the same mistake again.

99. They warn that self-change is dangerous, and hope that you don't see that listening to *them* is the danger.

100. Be alert to thought-voices that want you to think that impulsive spending of money is fun.

101. They wear you out by telling you how sincere they are, while laughing at your suppressed fear of their treachery.

102. You need never again obey a voice that orders you to feel lost and helpless in life.

TRUTH BANISHES LONELINESS

103. Loneliness exists only because the voices send false information about an individual's relationship with Truth.

104. One speaker specializes in making evil look like good, as when it glorifies suffering.

105. Be wide awake to the harmful voice that tricks you into thinking that you *already understand yourself and life.*

106. Stop the voice which talks you into doing favors for others which cost you money and time and regret.

107. One way they assault someone is to talk him into stormy likes and dislikes, which destroy clear thinking.

108. Good and helpful voices are never absent, but awareness of them must be strengthened by refusing harmful voices.

DISMISS A HARMFUL LIFE

109. You dismiss wrong people and events by seeing how hard the voices work to attract a wrong life to you.

110. The voices try to distract you from the present task at hand, which is the cause of inefficiency and accidents.

111. They tell you that life is not worth living, but it can become a valuable life when they are not living through you.

112. Unwanted habits fade away as the harmful mental voices fade away, for the voices encourage the habits.

113. You are now learning to say *NO* to the voices which tempt you to fall victim to pressure tactics from people.

114. They place doubts about yourself along the path, but you need only walk past them as if they are fallen leaves.

A POWERFUL TRUTH

115. *They* are insane, but lie and call *you* insane, so remember that *they* are not *you,* so you have only your truly sane self.

116. One voice is like a sadistic prison guard who encourages a prisoner to speak his mind, then punishes him for doing so.

117. They are fully capable of speaking in the name of God, which explains all the horrors committed by mechanical religion.

118. Worried when someone approaches their hiding place, they howl out a distraction, like lying that true life is a dull life.

119. A voice may first probe around and slyly ask questions of an intended victim, seeking for a weak spot to assault.

120. Quietly reject their loud demands that you listen to their folly, for you owe them nothing.

THE CURE FOR NERVOUSNESS

121. Any time you get nervous it is only because you carelessly listen to a voice that demands that you get nervous.

122. It makes no difference what a person does with his life as long as he ignores the fact of his surrender to evil voices.

123. They urge you to be a winner in life, but don't reveal that they mean an ego-win by which they can continue to use you.

124. To prevent you from finding present happiness they praise the fine times you had before things became rough.

125. Defending false positions is a major cause of human agony, so no longer let the swindling speakers do this through you.

126. They have a frantic fear of anyone who has determined to place Truth first and last in his life.

YOUR CORRECT ANSWER

127. When a voice tearfully complains that you are not putting it *first,* you should firmly reply that you are putting it *out.*

128. They love to lecture about loyalty, hoping that you don't see that they mean loyalty to foolish beliefs.

129. Sometimes they attack one after another, as when a man weakened by gloomy words is next accused of cowardice.

130. Millions of people fall for their trickery when they call organized public stupidity a noble and inspiring ceremony.

131. They preach that you must love everyone, then condemn you as cold and selfish when you can't.

132. Don't worry if you don't know how to handle sinister speakers, for Truth knows and will teach any sincere student.

VICTORY THROUGH SELF-INSIGHT

133. If pained by a voice that says that others don't understand you, realize that self-understanding stops that voice.

134. They talk a man right off the edge of a cliff by telling him that a cliff is not a cliff.

135. Mob hysteria and violence occurs when sheep-like human beings all agree to obey the same ruthless and stupid voice.

136. No lie causes more needless pain than the falsehood that results must turn out the way you demand.

137. They want you to think that you are irritated with yourself, when in fact you are unhappy with their presence.

138. When you ignore a villainous voice it fears defeat, so guarantee its collapse by refusing it attention.

WHAT THE VOICES CONCEAL

139. Mental pain occurs when personal fantasy collides with spiritual fact, but the voices don't want you to see this.

140. They tell a man that the world owes him success, then when others reject his claim they tell him to hate the world.

141. Never tolerate any voice that laughs at you after an embarrassing incident, but start life over at each new moment.

142. Observing the common practice of talking to oneself is a good start for understanding harmful voices.

143. They praise a man's yearning for gold and glory but never mention his higher yearning for inner wholeness.

144. When people threaten and pressure you the good voices will give you true power over their vicious voices.

SEE THROUGH THIS TRICK

145. If they can confuse someone into thinking that a *belief* is the same as a *fact* they have him where they want him.

146. They praise a neurotic person of the opposite sex in a sick attempt to make him or her seem desirable.

147. An evil voice will scream horribly if it senses that you are beginning to listen to a sane voice.

148. Unpleasant people are simply those who obey voices that call wrong right and call right wrong.

149. They sneak in through absent-mindedness, turn a man toward destruction, then sneak out and wait for the next chance.

150. Their power is fixed and mechanical, so you can leave them as easily as you walk away from a noisy cement mixer.

DON'T FEEL ASHAMED

151. They snicker about sex in a way that scares or embarrasses you, trying to make you feel ashamed of yourself.

152. Capable of quick costume-change, they appear friendly and helpful one moment, then suddenly switch to slandering you.

153. They love to get someone engaged in ego-competition, knowing that the fight will be followed by fear and depression.

154. Many voices offer delusory religious hope, then cruelly drain the unaware victim's very life.

155. They sneer at anything good and true and urge you to do the same, hoping to drag you down to their low level.

156. Weariness with life will change to cheer and command just as fast as you get rid of the hostile voices.

THE GREAT SECRET

157. The entire secret of freedom is in knowing who you are from yourself, not from what imposter-voices say you are.

158. False voices give foolish advice on sex problems, but they can be replaced by wise voices with healthy counsel.

159. Demons know the power of dressing well and appearing respectable when they denounce others as being demons.

160. When they slander your intelligence you should simply realize that your true wisdom is far above your usual mind.

161. They convince most people that the popular or familiar course is the right course, which is why most people suffer.

162. Each refusal to fear the threat of a black-mailing speaker makes the next voice weaker.

REFUSE THIS THREAT

163. Practice at catching a thought-voice that threatens you with loss of any kind, then refuse to fear its message.

164. One of the most dangerous voices of all is the one that tells you that anger is good and protective.

165. Worry over your inability to cast out demon voices is exactly what they want, so leave this task to powerful Truth.

166. They tremble when you begin to think of them as nothing but bad habits which you can break.

167. Millions love the voice which blames others for their griefs, which is why millions continue to suffer.

168. Freedom from harmful voices is like leaving a noisy street to arrive in a quiet and colorful meadow.

YOUR ACTIONS FOR SELF-HEALING

The truths you have collected can now start to work for you in daily conditions. Just turn them loose and you will see how powerful and practical they are.

They will help you in every area of life. They will supply peace and command in human relations, provide an understanding of love and sex, show you how to solve problems swiftly, and give your life real meaning and purpose.

Carry this publication with you to work and other places away from home. Read a few lines and then glance around at the world of people surrounding you. Notice how clearly these truths describe men and women as they really are. See how everyone is victimized by his own false voices.

A specific method for daily progress is to make mental or written notes of harmful voices you detect in yourself and others. Each new detection adds inner strength.

Read the following facts several times so that you will never forget them. The vicious voices will hatefully attack the truths in this publication, calling them cruel and unloving. But it is *they* who are cruel and unloving, and fear exposure of this fact. Darkness hates light. Their violence against these facts is just another sick trick of theirs to keep you under their obnoxious influence. *Their angry rejection is perfect proof of the trueness of these teachings.* An astonishing and healthy revelation will one day appear to you. The evil voices will give themselves away right before your very eyes. It will be like the seemingly gentle Dr. Jekyll turning into the wicked Mr. Hyde.

A glance at human behavior proves the need for a new spiritual lamp. That lamp is the wisdom in the publication you now hold in your hands. It tells the truth about the human condition and reveals the truth about the permanent cure.

Have no concern if other people do not want these rescuing realities. Give full attention to your own journey toward the brighter life. You see, when you wish a higher way for yourself you have obeyed the spiritual law of personal growth. Your reward will truly be out of this world.

Remain cheerful! You have every reason to maintain a sunny nature. For what action is more pleasant than walking toward authentic happiness? Be further encouraged by realizing that the energy wasted by foreign voices will now be channeled toward a new life.

Discover a new life—that is what life is really all about. You have already made a fine start in the right direction. Walk on!

• • •

Chapter 7

100 Ways to Defeat Satan

The world is enough to drive you crazy—but you don't have to go. You can win. You can win everything you need to win. Defeat is unnecessary because higher guidance is possible.

Your reading will result in two main revelations:

1. Methods for understanding everything about evil.
2. Methods for defeating Satan and finding True Life.

Your supreme advantage over evil spirits and horrible humans is your knowledge about them. Man is like a forged painting on a museum wall which thousands of viewers believe is real. But you will be like a skilled detective whose perception reveals it as false. Perception is power.

Your knowledge about evil leads you into right action for defeating it. You will use powerful exercises for banishing all that is threatening and harmful. These spiritual exercises are as interesting as a parade and as practical as bread.

As you proceed, remember that one part of you will enthusiastically love these higher guides, but another part will not fully understand them at first. No problem. Just relax and continue to march forward. An idea may play around the edges of your mind for awhile, but will finally enter to become a guiding light. Everyone goes through this preliminary stage of the journey and exits with smiles.

Here is a rule that becomes a valued prize for all who follow it earnestly: *See through others by first seeing through yourself.* So be pleased when self-study reveals you to be different than you believed! This is exactly what lifts you to higher levels each day. So study yourself boldly. Just be more curious than you are timid. That will do it.

Truth is *for* human beings because it is *against* the hostile forces that occupy them. So any time you feel that these teachings are too harsh, remember that they are not harsh toward you, but against the very worries that you want to dismiss. This is the perfect partnership—Truth and you, working together for all that is good.

To defeat evil you must see something that few do. See that nothing is more useful than to devote yourself to the power higher than you. Want a noble nature more than you want sex and sex cannot bother you. Want contentment more than excitement and nervousness is impossible. Loneliness, weakness and all else fall before the invited higher power. All this happens because God is all and evil is nothing.

Every week a young man asked his father to advise him on his griefs with girls, money and all else. His father finally said, "Look, son, why don't you ask for advice *before* getting into trouble?" Good advice for anyone, any age.

Your mind can operate in one of two ways: 1. As a tyrant that cruelly drives you through your day. 2. As a receiver of higher impressions. Take a close look. How do you classify your mind? Is it driven or does it flow?

If you don't like the punishment of tyranny along the way, you don't have to continue along that way. There is a new route with attractive scenery and a delightful final destination. For example, you may now believe you are worried over another person's opinion of you. That is not the problem at all. What bothers you is what *you* think about what *he* thinks. So the tyrant is your own unnecessary self-concern, for what he thinks about you has absolutely no relationship to your personal happiness. This kind of realization can expel all mental tyrants.

Higher impressions are spiritual truths and facts that wish to come down and help you. Knowing what you really need, their supply is ready and generous. For instance, they know what human beings are really like and want to tell you. These higher truths warn you against people who claim they have something good for you. The truth is, these deceivers really want to twist your life for their own profit and pleasure. They don't reveal their selfish motives, but Truth does. Each time you listen to these higher impressions your day becomes easier.

Realize that the higher understands the lower. You can be like a forest ranger on a mountain peak who looks down and knows just what to do to put out a fire. The fire will go out.

Like to have all problems solved for you? Like to live above the terrors of this world? Like to have something to do that is always fun? Like to be sure of yourself always? Like to have a treasure that will last forever? Like to go through your day without feeling threatened by anything? Like to discover a way to live casually and pleasantly? If so, here is all you have to do.

Have affection for Truth.

INSPIRING ANSWERS

Q. What do I fear most of all?

A. You fear the loss of your present existence— your imaginary existence made up of all your past thoughts and experiences. But believing it is real, you fear its loss. God cannot be the author of this anxiety, so Satan is. Lose mental existence and win Spiritual Existence.

Q. How do these studies put us at ease in home life and business affairs?

A. When an evil force is banished inwardly it loses all power outwardly. When there is nothing anxious inside there is nothing distressful outside.

Q. Why do we stumble from one meaningless relationship or activity to the next?

A. *Different* is not *new*, but everyone wants to think so.

171

Q. *What would happen if I attended a lecture by a True Teacher?*

A. You would realize that for the first time in your life you heard a speaker who did not lie to you. You must then decide between the offered Truth and your old ways.

Q. *How does insight conquer fear?*

A. Keep people at a distance, not because you fear they are vicious but because you know they are.

Q. *What is the explanation of human devils who seem fond of each other?*

A. The reason they like each other is because they are like each other. Evil loves evil. Society is a gang of friendly phonies who finally attack each other.

Q. *Is it simply self-deception when I think that I or anyone else makes intelligent decisions?*

A. What is called making an intelligent decision is nothing but yielding to the course which gives maximum personal reward. There is no intelligence or goodness or courage involved— only concealed self-interest.

Q. *How do you explain the brutal ambition of some people for power and tyranny in society?*

A. If you want to be a leader at the zoo you must first be one of the animals.

Q. May I hear something helpful that I don't want to hear?

A. The average human being is nothing but a small child who can't take care of himself. When hurt he cries, when promised a lollipop he beams with pleasure. These are the people who are running things.

Q. How can I be freely natural?

A. Ask yourself if pain is good or bad. You will then lie and say it is bad, for you always answer the way that sounds sincere. But your pain-nature thinks it is good, for it loves itself and wants to keep you in its pain. Let your true nature see that pain is bad.

Q. Devils seem to have a certain kind of evil glee, but what is it?

A. They put their faith in the incompetence of human society to solve its problems—and are never disappointed. Human devils thrive on human disorder.

Q. What is the difference between stupidity and intelligence?

A. Stupidity wants to glorify itself, while intelligence wants more of itself.

Q. Why do I always have enemies?

A. Because you get a false and destructive pleasure in having enemies. You *want* them. If you don't believe it, just try giving up an enemy. Go ahead, right now. Try to stop seeing him as an enemy. See? You still have the enemy you want.

Q. *What causes anger?*

A. Anger erupts when personal phoniness is exposed. The captured crook always hates the policeman.

Q. *How can I recognize a false teacher when I see one?*

A. Watch him like a hawk. Notice his concealed nervousness, his pretense of confidence, his suppressed anger. Nothing is easier to see *providing you really want to see him in all his hideous hypocrisy.*

Q. *How can people be so wicked and yet appear so happy?*

A. Because evil is their entertainment, in fact, doing sick things is a human's single most popular amusement. Your refusal to admit this puts you in danger from humans.

Q. *What is panic?*

A. A false solution. It is like trying to unlock a door with a hammer. You do the wrong thing simply because you don't know the right thing. Patient study reveals the right.

Q. How can I understand true freedom?

A. See what it is *not*. Psychopaths scream that they are free.

Q. What should I do when I don't know what to do about family strife, financial problems, about all else?

A. You don't have to do *anything* unless directed to do so by the Spirit of Truth. Satan lies and tells you that the intellect can know what to do. You cannot *think* of what to do, but through the Spirit of Truth you can *know*. This defeats Satan and anxiety.

Q. No doubt I am stupid toward Satan and the human sickness he causes, but what can be done?

A. See that stupidity is not the problem. The refusal of intelligence about life is the problem. Look how you fight learning. Relax and receive.

Q. I suspect that the world is more evil than I see, but how do I attain full realization?

A. What you cannot now see with your mental eyes you will one day see through spiritual vision. Spiritual eyes can see evil as clearly as your usual eyes now see a house.

GUIDES TO SUCCESS

To win happiness, see 42, 51, 57, 61, 88.

To solve problems, see 6, 25, 37, 44, 64.

To detect deceit, see 2, 16, 19, 31, 58.

To use exercises, see 8, 30, 52, 60, 94.

To discover peace, see 14, 18, 26, 56, 81.

To understand love, see 17, 63, 66, 97, 98.

To command life, see 23, 24, 68, 92, 100.

To be protected, see 15, 21, 50, 65, 96.

To manage people, see 10, 33, 43, 49, 70.

To banish anxiety, see 22, 39, 41, 73, 74.

To feel refreshed, see 5, 38, 47, 82, 86.

To build strength, see 4, 9, 55, 78, 80.

To end confusion, see 40, 75, 76, 77, 93.

To avoid attacks, see 7, 71, 72, 84, 89.

To heal hurts, see 11, 27, 48, 54, 95.

To develop insight, see 3, 20, 29, 35, 36.

To escape evil, see 28, 32, 62, 79, 91.

To live naturally, see 12, 13, 53, 83, 85.

To stop depression, see 46, 59, 67, 87, 90.

To find guidance, see 1, 34, 45, 69, 99.

1. SECRET COMMAND   A story was written about an army general who knew every move the enemy army was making. He was in command of the enemy because he had obtained their secret orders. You are now obtaining the plans that will place you in charge of *everything* that tries to hurt you. It can be called Superwisdom. One way to acquire Superwisdom is to try to see higher than your present *wants*. What you now want is not all there is!

2. SATAN UNMASKED   Satan is: a. Any thought, feeling or action performed unconsciously. b. Ignorance of God and spiritual Truths. c. Hatred of all that is truly good and decent and healthy. d. The same as being insane, psychopathic, paranoid, egotistical. e. Anything harmful to anyone, such as cruelty, slander, deception. f. Lying by calling evil good and good evil. All these inner states express themselves outwardly in crime, violence, misery. You need not be part of it.

3. SATANIC POSSESSION   The devil enters, possesses and operates through human beings. He is an invisible force that commands human minds and bodies. His survival depends upon keeping his slaves ignorant of this fact. For example, a devil-possessed man will hatefully deny his fiendish condition, which is the very devil's lying denial. Satan anxiously fears being expelled from an awakening human being, for Satan's victim has been his home.

4. YOUR CASTLE Remember that working *for yourself* is exactly the same as working *against Satan.* The powers that build your inner strength also demolish your inner weakness. So have no fear if you feel a sense of loss as you work inwardly. You are losing what has caused you to lose. The more you lose the more you win. You lose the haunted house in order to build a shining castle in its place. This is an exciting secret for changing your inner residence. Move today.

5. EMPTY LIVES If you could see the awful emptiness of human lives you would be shocked speechless. But you must not hesitate to see it, for here is your chance to flee what you see, to finally find self-wholeness. The average man's idea of happiness is to sit around and look important with the least amount of effort. What others may choose, you must refuse. Society is incurably insane. Choose personal spiritual sanity. Sanity is charming.

6. SEX WORLD The sex center is highly emotional, therefore a major target for hostile spirits. Their aim is to torment the victim with guilt and frustration. They do this by urging a man to merely think about sex, to indulge in sex fantasies in which he shares the bed of every pretty girl in town. His solution is to substitute learning for yearning. *He must voluntarily lose confidence in his fantasy world of sex.* He then enters a new world of natural command over sex.

7. USED PEOPLE   See a demon as a *user* of human beings. Watch an angry man. Notice how an invisible force uses and agitates his physical parts. His vocal chords send out snarling threats, his mouth twists weirdly, his eyes flash fire, and his arms and body jerk violently. You are seeing demon-possession in action. The angry man has been taken over. He is used, controlled, tyrannized. Still believe that people are self-controlled? Don't.

8. INNER EXERCISE   You must build your spiritual memory, which is awareness in action. Use this exercise to succeed. You now hold this publication at a certain page. Now, each time you turn a page be aware of yourself doing it. Instead of unseen mechanical action, *know* that your hand reaches to the page top, be *conscious* that the page turns. Determine to do this at each page—and notice how easily you forget! Your awareness of your unawareness is pure gold. Collect all you can.

9. SAVE ENERGY   Picture a power line running to your pleasant cabin in the woods. But all along the way some thieves have tapped into the line, stealing electricity. Power intended only for your personal use has been drained off for illegal purposes. The devil is an energy thief. He steals natural power by making people unhappy. Unhappiness is a dreadful drain of constructive energy. Ever see it like that? See it like that. It saves you.

179

10. STAGE ACT Don't feel sorry for weak people. Their pathetic appearance is a cunning stage performance. Don't be deceived. A weak and pathetic man is a dangerous man. Inwardly he boils with rage. He will destroy you if he can. A habitually drooping man has an equal chance to climb to inner strength, but he refuses it in favor of deceitful dependency. If you think you should feel compassion for the weak, remember this. The weak seek out the strong, not to learn but to steal.

11. END PUNISHMENT A man is punished by one thing only—his own low level of life-understanding. This means he is punished by the devil all right, but the devil is simply his own ignorance. His choice of stupidity is the same as his preference for mental hell. To escape he must stop seeing his hell as heaven. Do you know someone who loves hatred and revenge? That is his idea of heaven. His life can be described as an orgy of madness.

12. ROAD SIGNS A sure way to defeat Satan is to recognize the consistency of Truth. Truth cannot lie, never falters, is always the same bright light. Notice its consistent instructions to see hatred as self-destructive, to seek riches higher than the intellect. But falsehood is inconsistent, treacherous, and finally abandons you to your screams. Consistent truths are like road signs posted all the way through an unknown valley. You don't have to anxiously *think*—just *follow*.

13. MENTAL PICTURES A man does not live from himself, but from mental pictures about himself. He pictures himself as wise, loving, strong, and, of course, as always right. But it is these very imaginations that keep him stupid, hateful, weak, wrong. They separate him from the true virtues of Reality. Angry spirits operate through these fantasies. *Few people ever realize that self-pictures rule and ruin their lives.* Realize it. Your health will grow.

14. INNER PEACE Detach your inner world from the outer world. Your eyes see someone with whom you quarreled? Let your eyes alone be active, let your mind remain quiet. Your ears hear that someone slandered you? Let your ears only be active, let your spirit be still. Your inner Reality does not believe in outer appearances. Nothing forces you to admit a wolf into your home. You can stop trouble from entering any time you remember this. Remember this all day long.

15. CLEAR MESSAGE Mixing with people is mixing with their troubles. They will promptly try to make their misery your misery. They will lie and deny this evil, of course, for they refuse to see how low they are. A man with a brutal manner or a woman with a hateful face are trying to drag you into their sick world. Your new Spirit of Truth will send them an invisible message that speaks louder than a million words: "Stay out of my life."

16. A DESCRIPTION It is easy to describe anyone under the power of darkness. Nothing exists for him except the grabbing of worldly rewards. He especially hates anyone who exposes his actual childishness. One of his insanities is to think he can do wrong and feel right. He calls his disgrace innocence. His idea of heaven is to be surrounded by bright lights that reflect his own image. He fears to notice how much he is despised. He has the conscience of a shark.

17. TRUE LOVE No one cares for anyone. All is vanity. The evil that rules people cares for nothing but its own ruinous ways. The idea of people loving each other is a lie from sick human minds. A hypocrite hates this truth, for in his egotism he wants to see himself as loving. He can then demand rewards for himself. True love is from God. It comes to whoever finally sees that a self-picture of being loving is unloving. Love is above human thought.

18. STOP SATAN Fear attracts whatever is feared. Why? Because fear is ignorance, like a dazed man so fearful of falling into a swamp that he dizzily does so. Fear prophesies tragedy, then leads the terrified person toward its fulfillment. Spiritual wisdom dissolves time, which prevents the prophesied event from happening, which is the same as stopping the devil right now. *You cannot fear anything you understand.* You can understand and stop painful prophecies. Vigorously do so.

19. THE SWAMP Fake religious teachers and false religious followers love each other. Satan loves both. Teachers and followers love each other. Satan loves both. Teachers and followers have a lot in common, like vultures and buzzards. Each silently demands and gets soothing lies from the other, after which they all smilingly wander together down to the swamp. A sign of a truly unfolding spiritual life is to see through this devilish conspiracy. You cannot deceive a True Teacher. Be grateful for that.

20. SPIRITUAL PATH To discover the spiritual path you must drop all religious beliefs that say you are already on it. Spirituality and religion are as different as water and sand. God's light expresses spirituality, while man's darkness invents religion. The spiritual path cuts straight through the jungle of sick human nature. Avoidance of the path is avoidance of the Supreme Reason for being on earth. Whoever bravely follows the spiritual path to the very end will be saved. Bravely start.

21. PAY ATTENTION Hostile spirits like to cause grief by dividing and confusing your attention. Split attention is a major cause of accidents and inefficiency. When driving your car or handling tools, give full attention to the task, stay aware of your consecutive movements. This means to know what you are doing at the moment you are doing it, to remain with each action as it happens. Don't get ahead or in back of yourself. Results are rich.

22. STOP ANXIETY The devil uses anxiety like a soldier uses bullets—to wound and destroy. Anxiety is simply the result of a counterfeit life. Any life outside the spiritual world is counterfeit. There is no such thing as being spiritual and being anxious. There is definitely such a thing as being a fake and being anxious. The solution? No fakery, no fear. In this true state all anxious explanations are over. Happiness is to not have to explain yourself to yourself. This is a great relief.

23. HAUNTED HOUSE A movie hero was promised a rich inheritance for staying overnight in a haunted house. He fearfully endured the floating ghosts and flapping bats and sinister sounds. At dawn he received his inheritance. He then discovered that it was all a test, with mechanical monsters, to make sure he was a brave hero, worthy of the riches. Likewise, you will receive inner riches by enduring your own haunted house until dawn.

24. ACTIVE SATAN The devil does everything possible to prevent your discovery of a hideous fact about him. Desperately, he conceals the truth that he works through and among human beings. He wants you to think of him as dwelling in a remote hell, far removed from daily human activities. Don't believe it. Devils run governments, preach sermons, direct corporations, counsel neurotics, practice law, command armies, control education, establish charities, promote entertainment. Observe all this.

25. NEW MIND Maybe no one ever told you about this problem you have. You don't want to be where you are, doing what you are doing, mixing with people you really don't want around you. The only reason you are in this sad state is because you have not yet learned that an unwanted life is unnecessary. And this is because you insist upon taking orders from your present mind. You need a new mind. You can have it by letting yourself go. Let go.

26. SOCIAL MANIACS A suppressed and desperate cry surges through humanity. People shriek, "How can I make sense of human events?" You can't. The actions of lunatics in an insane asylum never make sense. Society is a madhouse occupied by frenzied maniacs who think they are sane. Sigh with relief. You don't have to try to figure it out any more. You can see through sick society, which means you are not part of it, which means you are sane. And now your life makes perfect sense.

27. THE HEALING Want to know why a man feels empty and frustrated? *He tells himself he can do something but finds he can't.* He says he can find fun in travel, but ends up bored and lonely. He informs himself that one day he will be loved and desired, but passing years deny his claim. All this comes as a furious blow to his vanity. Vanity can't do anything but hurt. For healing, he must stop talking to himself like that. This he can do.

28. THE LIES Satan advised some human beings who served him, "When anything threatens your self-interest, protect yourself with lies. No matter how many people you hurt, lie viciously. If accused of lying, scream back that your *accuser* is the liar. If disturbed by your own deceit, justify your lies by shouting that everyone does it. Remember that religious lies serve sickness best of all." Leaning over to his assistant, Satan whispered, "Now *those* stupid humans are destroyed."

29. STRONG TALK To see through wicked people it is needful to use strongly honest language. Don't think, "People are basically good, but are sometimes faulty." That is a self-serving evasion of the hard facts you don't want to see in yourself. See people with all the fierce savagery beneath their faked politeness. But do it scientifically, not self-righteously. This is the only way to shock yourself awake from life's nightmare. It is nice to wake up.

30. PASSING PARADE Stand on any busy corner. Select and look at any passing man. You will see a devil-possessed human being. Select any woman. Same thing. Both would laugh if told this, but it would be nervous scorn. Human life is a passing parade of pathetic paranoids. Nothing is different about them and nothing is worthwhile to them. They want to feel owned— and Satan obliges. Now they are victims. Now they want to make you one. Don't join the parade.

31. CLOSE LOOK Remember that a study of devil-nature is the same as a look at human nature. This means that a skilled student will not be bluffed by fakers. Behind the stern stare of a high authority is a mental defective. Behind the glowing smile is a woman who despises you. Behind strong leadership is a man who cries for his mama. Behind the considerate businessman is an insolent bum. Behind everyone else is a disgrace to the human race.

32. SATANIC SIGNS Ordinary thinking cannot recognize the devil when he appears. A man's usual mind is so loaded with weird self-interest he always takes demons for angels, as with smiling hypocrites. But you can learn to see signs of Satan—*which were in front of you all the time*. Aim to see evil as evil. See hateful glares as devilish, see insolence as insanity, see greed as depraved desire, see brutality as animalistic, see self-pity as self-sickness. Your right sight is your safety.

33. THE FACTS Some people are suspicious about praising and honoring people. Here are the facts. You praise a man for his strength and wisdom with the hope that your words will somehow magically change into his virtues, thus guaranteeing your own protection by him. This folly sponsors terrifying weakness and dependence upon delusion. It is also how Satan uses self-deceit to keep people shuffling through life with vacant eyes.

34. TRUE TEACHER   Once in awhile a True Teacher enters the world, a rare individual who has risen to the spiritual heights. He knows all about the devil, including the fact that Satan is nothing but a bundle of furious fakery. Nothing in life is hidden from a True Teacher, including the method by which you can save yourself. Having safely passed through the inner jungle himself, he can show you how to do the same. Want the same? You will find a True Teacher. He will welcome you.

35. SEE LIFE   To win real riches, ask yourself constantly, "Am I *thinking* or am I *seeing?*" They are completely different. Thinking consists of nervous ideas, while seeing consists of calm consciousness. Careless people mistake thinking for seeing, which keeps them hurting. Look at your mind. Do you see self-doubt, a nagging need to prove yourself right? That is useless thinking. Now you can learn to pleasantly see your way through life.

36. THE SLAVES   Some demons were cruelly tyrannizing dozens of human slaves who were miserably working in a hot desert. An amazed apprentice demon asked the chief demon, "But how do you keep them so contented?" The chief shrugged. "Easy. We just let them get used to slavery. Once it becomes familiar they ask no questions." Asked the apprentice, "But don't they fight to get out?" The chief laughed. "Don't be absurd. They fight anyone who tries to *help* them get out!"

37. THE CURSE Nothing is more stupid than self-trickery. It is a severely punishing curse. Millions foolishly believe they think for themselves. Few do. *To think for yourself is to live for yourself,* not for your fond fights. Do you fight a lot, including internal battles? Yes or no? If yes, you don't think for yourself but for everything that wrecks life. But what self-trickery started, self-wisdom can end. How nice to have this healing medicine!

38. YOUR PLEASURE Ever notice something about your human relationships? Those you want to come into your life are those who stay out, while those you wish to stay out are those who come in. Maddening? Anyone caught in this is at the mercy of *their* wishes, while he wants them to be at the mercy of *his* wishes. Conflict vanishes as you live from yourself, not from a false belief that others can reward you. Now, your pleasure is to let others come or go at their pleasure.

39. THE SWITCH Satan is always in a losing position. Your growing awareness will reveal this inspiring fact to you. Satan is like a television set gone crazy, in which scary scenes and sick sounds flash violently back and forth. All you need do is turn off the switch. Just as a television set depends on outside electricity, Satan depends upon your unconscious cooperation. Withdraw your consent to being scared. Ask Truth to turn off the switch. It will.

40. HUMAN STUPIDITY Satan and stupidity must be studied together, for evil and ignorance relate closely. Badness is madness. Stupidity is the absence of *spiritual* wisdom. A man can run his business adequately and still be spiritually stupid. A stupid person does not see himself as stupid, which makes him a typically horrible human being. His mind is stuffed with useless clippings from yesterday's news, which he proudly calls his library. Intelligence starts with awareness of personal stupidity.

41. FALSE FEAR People ask, "How can I stop fearing the devil?" The answer is both startling and liberating. Your own fear-thoughts create a mental picture of the devil which you then believe. *You believe the devil into existence—a false existence.* He has no power outside your own mistaken mind. You simply fear the word *devil* and all its fearful associative thoughts. Believe no more. The devil will be no more. Fear will be no more.

42. BE HAPPY It is useless to think about what will make you happy. If you think you know a source of sunshine you will try to find it in other people, in ownership, in effort and time. But these areas have never made anyone happy. You are happy when you don't think about happiness, for true peace cannot come from a strained mind. Anxious desire builds an illusory castle which collapses with the first frustration. Above all ideas about happiness is Happiness. Prove this for yourself.

43. AVOID TROUBLE   Avoid people who: a. Approach you with sad eyes. b. Display emotional love. c. Vow to behave better. d. Mention their past good deeds. e. Know what you need. f. Stand up for their rights. g. Try to involve you. h. Feel persecuted. i. Want to show you something. j. Have had bad breaks. k. Tell you to trust them. l. Are excited over great plans. m. Feel hurt at your refusal. n. Stare but don't see. o. Work hard to convince you.

44. USELESS GUILT   People easily fall under guilt when accused. Sly Satan sees to that. But it is human carelessness that allows this enemy-emotion. Strangely, a man *wants* to feel guilty. Why? Because it supports his strong but wrong belief of being the center of the world. With fiery feelings he assures himself, "I may be guilty and bad, but at least I am *someone*." But that does not make him someone, for an emotion does not create an identity. Do not mistake heat for light.

45. SUNNY LAND   Human life is hell on earth because everyone senses the emptiness of earthly riches and fame, but does not know the alternative. It is like a young boy living in a dark jungle who catches a single glimpse of a sunny land across a wide river. As he grows up he works and plays in the jungle but his heart is not in it. He yearns to cross the river. So do you. You can. Guided by the Spirit of Truth, you can reach the sunny land.

191

46. YEARNING EYES The devil delights in forcing people to look around for approval. Anyone living under dark influences is compelled to suffer the daily distress of seeking acceptance from others. His yearning eyes plead, "Please say you like me." Millions deny they are under this hypnotic spell. They are the very ones Satan tricks most easily. Total solution: Stop seeking approval for who you are *not*. You are not someone who needs approval. Ponder this deeply.

47. FEEL GOOD Man stumbles through life simply because he fails to notice the difference between fantasy and fact. One difference is that fantasy hurts and fact feels good. Practice this healing exercise by asking yourself every day, "How come my rightness feels so wrong?" Your aim is to expose and dismiss false rightness which always feels wrong. Pretense of trueness is painful. You can learn from what is true or you can burn from what is you.

48. ETERNAL LIFE One day a demon saw a man lose some money in his business. The demon urged him, "Go ahead, feel depressed, it's only natural." But the man ignored the demon. The next day the demon saw the man get crowded off the road by a reckless driver. The demon whispered, "Blow up in anger—it's your right." But the man remained calm. The demon did not know that the man wanted eternal life more than he wanted temporary egotistical feelings. Be like him.

49. VITAL POINT A chief trait of a human devil is his unawareness that he is one. You can pile his evil deeds a mile high in front of him and he still won't see them. Beware. He is a man without a soul. But like all devils he is so incredibly stupid that any sincere person can see what he is. Just see the insanity he refuses to see. For example, he is compelled to hatefully accuse others of evil, so that by contrast he appears innocent. See through him.

50. FALSE TEACHER It is easy to expose a false religious teacher who is controlled by compulsive evil. Just let someone tell him that he is a religious hypocrite and watch his reaction. In one way or another he will react with nervous hostility. Think carefully. Would a True Teacher get upset if told he was false? Not at all. *He knows who he is.* But a false teacher falls into anger because he knows that his identity as a religious teacher is a fake. He fears and hates getting exposed.

51. HOME SAFE A young prince foolishly left the safety of his father's castle to roam recklessly and dangerously around. He finally wanted to go home, but shame stood in his way. His father sent him a message which could not be understood clearly at first because of blurred ink, but the prince finally read: *Just come home.* Likewise, one day you will fully understand and accept Truth's invitation. The reckless roaming is no more. You are home safe.

52. CATCH PRETENDERS You are hurt by what you don't know about human nature. Use this exercise for correction. Wherever you go, study human ways to notice sly stunts and hidden motives. Concentrate on catching pretenses. Everyone has his specialties. As you watch people in public, inform yourself, "He is pretending to be innocent." Or, "She is pretending to be loving." To expose and defeat human pretense is the same as defeating Satan. Double his defeats.

53. NEW LIFE You can actually become a new kind of human being. The great secret of success is to throw yourself upon your own resources 100 times. Nothing will happen. Throw yourself upon yourself 1000 times. Nothing will change. Try it 5000 times. Nothing will be different. Try it 5001 times. Something will happen. You will start a new and rich life far above both your own mind and the madness of human society. Start now.

54. CONCEALED DANGER Treacherous Lucifer prevents millions from seeing this fact: your own present ways make you a danger to yourself. By keeping people anxious toward external foes, such as false friends or financial stress, he blocks their sighting of the actual danger—their own wrong inner conditions. Can you see *your* weakness as *your* danger? Can you see *your* self-excusing as *your* barrier to self-command? If not, do so starting today. Self-danger will fade.

55. DEVIL'S DISCIPLE   Satan loves and encourages imaginary victories. They serve his purpose perfectly. A man who chooses fantasy over fact can hide out in his dark little room of delusions and let fancy roam wherever it likes. Does he wish to be the great lover of every pretty girl he sees? Imagination creates the lover. Does he want to avoid unpleasant facts about himself? In mental scenes he is charming. Satan observes, smiles. Good student.

56. THE ARGUER   There was once a man who was called the Arguer. He argued over everything, just to give himself the false thrill of emotional electricity. Taken over by a violent spirit, he argued to convince himself, not others. His compulsive quarreling tore him down and wore him out. One day he heard a short message that freed him from his tormenting need to fight. He heard, "Just don't argue. Nothing bad will happen to you." He saw it was true. What a revelation!

57. VICTORY NOW   Satan is *already defeated.* He trembles that you may see this. You need not fight Satan personally, but just realize that God has already won the battle. It is like a dazed soldier fighting wearily on in the jungle, not knowing that his nation won the war years ago! Defeat consists only of *not realizing* this astounding fact. You win this victory-through-understanding by rising above time-thinking to dwell in the Spiritual Now.

58. RELIGIOUS HYPOCRITES Operating and degenerating within the Satanic circle, a religious hypocrite is sub-human. His hideous purpose in life is to hatefully attack and destroy all that is truly godly and good. Quoting mechanically from religious books, he proudly asks others if they are as saved as his sick mind says he is. Self-tormented, he slyly torments and confuses those he pretends to help. You can't shame him, for he has no shame, only monstrous arrogance.

59. CONQUER PAIN An event or condition is harmless and neutral unless it is stopped by the intellect which operates in opposites. Two such opposites are, "Will that event help or hurt me?" and "Can I or can't I win an ego-victory in this argument?" When stopped by either side, an event becomes either pleasurable pain or painful pain. To conquer mental pain, stand aside and let an event pass through the mind filled with opposites and go on to pure insight.

60. USE TELEVISION People dwell under the strange hypnosis of daily life. You can use television as a powerful exercise to break the spell and wake up. Notice how you become personally involved with an exciting movie or the evening news. You react with pleasure or pain at what you see. From now on, deliberately and constantly turn your head away from the screen and *become aware of yourself as a viewer, not a participant.* Detach yourself. Be separate. You are waking up!

61. HIGHER RESULTS A thought or act is a cause that produces a result that is like the cause. If you dip a brush into red paint the brush will turn red, even if you hope for green. On the negative side of this law, self-fascination results in a wasted life. On the positive side, a love for inner-development results in enduring vitality. Evil produces evil and good produces good. To enrich what happens to you, build a new you. It is a pleasant task.

62. THE PROOF Want proof that human beings are devils in disguise? Well, name a few traits of the devil. *Concealed hatred. Deceitful words. Vicious attacks. False goodness.* Right? Right. Now, name a few traits of human beings. *Concealed hatred. Deceitful words. Vicious attacks. False goodness.* Right? Right. So a man is *exactly the same* as a devil. The servants of Satan despise this unmasking. But they can't escape its pure proof of the monsters that they really are.

63. POWERFUL PLAN Use this simple but powerful weapon for defeating the devil. What Satan loves, you must unlove. The devil loves brooding depression and senseless schemes. Unlove these. Satan sends out hideous thoughts about hurting and conquering people. Unlove such ideas when they try to enter your mind. Simply love the opposite of what the devil loves. You will feel the opposite of anguish, which is peace and intelligence.

64. FALSE PROBLEMS No problem is a problem to you. It is a problem to the two states involved in a desire. The first state is your desire for wealth. The second state is your thought about lack of wealth. So there is conflict and pain. But you are neither the desire for wealth nor the idea about lack of wealth. Your truly spiritual nature dwells far above all contradictory ideas. Let your pondering of this turn into realization. You will then see that all problems are false problems.

65. FIERY FACTORY When dealing with a human devil, remember this. He cannot react toward you except with *more* deviltry. He can give you only what he is—evil. Outwardly he may appear pleasant and cooperative, but behind the sly smile his fiery mental factory is already manufacturing his next betrayal of you. Ignorance of this causes pain. Now, you can either refuse this fact or let it rescue you. Wisely select rescue.

66. THE FEW Each day hundreds of lost and fearful people lined up in front of a True Teacher. The wise man could see through all of them at a glance. Each approached to ask, "Can you show me how to stop destroying myself?" For days at a time the Teacher answered only, "No, because you will not let me." But every once in awhile an inquirer heard, "Yes, because you will let me." The Teacher saw that a few had the necessary sincerity to walk toward spiritual light. Be one of the few.

67. HALFWAY HELL Malicious spirits eagerly trap people in a halfway hell. The torment starts when one part of you wants to do something but another part objects. You start an exciting drive to somewhere, but halfway there your mind changes and you yearn to stop. You battle between go and stop, with both sides equally insistent. You are caught between two lying promises of self-security. Spiritual wholeness will break the ache. Travel to wholeness.

68. BE WHOLE A man must see that he is in trouble with himself. With that healthy awareness he can start sailing toward a new world. So it is just fine to find something wrong, as long as you start with yourself. To awaken awareness of wrongness, just see that you can't escape your own screaming mind, that your thoughts can't cure your thoughts. This shatters delusions of having self-control. Self-awareness of self-weakness supplies self-wholeness. You are above yourself.

69. EASY LIFE Like to toss off the burdens that paranoid people drop into your lap? Simple. Just be an inwardly right human being. You see, wrongness is a chain that connects you with the consequences of human evil, such as painful punishment and corrupt conditions. Personal trueness breaks the chain, changes you from an outer-controlled person to inner-controlled. Life is easy when *you* are not right but *Right* is right. Make it easy.

70. NEW CLUE The average person is contemptuous toward anyone he cannot deceive
or manipulate. Ignore this fact at your own
peril. Let it be a new clue for your daily safety.
Quietly observe a man who tries to exploit
you. Watch how he gives himself away when
you finally refuse him. Coming out into the open,
he snarls at you like a cornered weasel. Think
this is too strong against human beings? You
have not even seen the start of human horror.
Your sight is strength.

71. THE REASON The reason people can hurt
you is because they are more cruel than you think.
The reason humans can deceive you is because
they are more treacherous than you know. The
reason men can corrupt you is because they are
more devilish than you believe. The reason
women can enslave you is because they are more
oppressive than you see. Think from these facts,
not from foolish beliefs. You will fly away free.

72. HUMAN DEVIL Here are three ways to
identify a devil in human form. a. He can charge
like an insane bull to break and hurt people,
but you must not criticize his behavior with
one small word. b. It is his majestic privilege to
grab whatever he wants when he wants it, but
your wishes must await his royal permission.
c. He has a perfect right to scream furiously
when his demands are thwarted, but you have no
right to ask him to behave with normal courtesy.
Watch for these devils.

73. PERFECT PLAN Here is a plan that will stop distress when you don't know how to stop distress. 1. Notice clearly that you are in fact distressed. *2. Stop right there.* By going beyond awareness you wrongly refer the problem to your usual intellect. This intellect cannot solve the problem because it caused the distress in the first place. A raging storm cannot calm itself. Your *noticing without thinking* permits higher insight to understand *for* you.

74. DIABOLIC DECEIT Here is the single most diabolical deception by which Satan enslaves humanity. Lying, he tells a man that he possesses an independent self apart from God. The foolish man is then convinced that he is his name, his experiences, his pains and pleasures. Egotistical man believes the lie because his immature mind likes to cast him in the role of a hero operating on his own. This blocks his entrance into the One Kingdom, which delights Satan. Don't delight Satan.

75. THE ZOO How would you describe your mental activities? One man described his mind as "A zoo gone mad with shrieking and clawing beasts." He was describing his sudden explosions of worry and frustration. A bored and unhappy person is always *looking for an excuse to turn loose his mental zoo,* just to give himself a few exciting minutes. Absolute horror! You must have none of this. Don't yield to excuses. Your mind was not meant to be a zoo.

76. FREE SPEECH Do you have speech problems? Maybe you stutter or speak nervously. Perhaps you don't know what to say or fear talking before an audience. This simply indicates confusion in your inner system, which sends wrong instructions up to your speech centers. It is like a faulty traffic signal that makes the lights flash wrongly. The wisdom in these pages will correct all this. You will learn to speak clearly, wisely, with decision and finality. This is fine self-work.

77. END FEAR Millions fear failure in self-rescue. This torment is just another Satanic stunt to keep you out of the kingdom. Fear arises from man's false personality and is therefore false itself. Of course the false self can't save itself—nonexistence can't do anything! So this agonizing fear is simply the needless agitation of ignorance and imagination. *You save yourself by seeing there is no one here who needs to be saved.* Let this become clear to you.

78. INSTANT HELP The usual mind cannot win over Satan, for his dark forces occupy and command an undeveloped mind. But you can choose to yield your present mind to the Spirit of Truth, who will send immediate help. Go ahead and doubt your present mind all you want, for it is spiritually unreliable, having no power to fly upward. This is constructive doubt. So leave the usual mind on earth, and learn to fly high. Finally, all doubts will disappear.

79. FALSE WORSHIP   People believe they worship God. Pure delusion. They build their preferred kind of god out of their own anxious beliefs and greeds. Imagination supplies the god they want—one who permits them to hide their own violence from themselves. A man's egotism can't lose with this fantasy-god who lovingly looks down to see him as persecuted and innocent. This self-worship is devil-worship. It is also religious insanity.

80. THE QUESTION   A dozen demons from hell conspired to attack a True Teacher. One at a time the demons attacked with blasphemous shrieks of contempt. They clawed with threats of destruction. Standing calmly, the Teacher waited until each demon drooped with exhaustion from his own violence. The Teacher then asked a demon, "Which one of us is suffering agonizing punishment from his own depravity—you or me?" Shocked and defeated, each demon slunk away, cursing.

81. SHOCK WAVES   You reach God by deliberately passing through a series of spiritual shock waves. These walloping waves occur when you refuse to dodge unpleasant facts about yourself. So just stand there and permit a collision between your beloved beliefs toward yourself and the frank facts about yourself. Devils posing as saints won't do this, for it would expose their hypocrisy. You do it. You won't suffer from hypocrisy. You will live in light.

82. FRESH LIFE Have some practical fun. Write down all the strong points you think you possess. You might believe you welcome new truths, are decisive, know what you want, and so on. Now, ponder each point carefully. *Compare it with your daily ways.* Feel nervous? Sense something wrong? Good! The more distress you see the better. You are now aware of the nervousness in self-contradiction, which makes you want to stop it. This is how others won a fresh life. Win your own.

83. DISAPPEARING DEVIL The devil vanishes to the same degree that personal egotism vanishes. They are the same. Egotism is repulsive. So is Satan. Egotism feels secret pleasure in hurting others. So does the devil. Egotism storms with rage when thwarted. So does an evil spirit. So whoever wants to end a life of anguish can do so by simply dropping useless egotism. Millions fearfully refuse to believe all this. You can see it—and flourish.

84. THE COWARD Somewhere in this world there is a cowardly man. He hides his cowardice with bluffing behavior. All he really wants is to grab and run. He is a deluded roamer, trying to find health in his own sickness. Anyone who even comes close to exposing his cowardice is viciously slandered. He despises anything that is truly good and constructive. He associates only with others who are as cowardly as himself. You now have a description of the average human being. See it.

85. PURE FACT   There exists the fact of what is right and what is wrong. But ego-serving human belief distorts the pure fact. Belief arises in a lost human being who stupidly prefers his belief to the fact. His chance for self-rescue from self-evil is to simply see that his personal belief about right and wrong is not the pure fact about right and wrong. To do this he must see that his belief is ruining him. This fact is right in front of him.

86. SENSELESS SCENES   Satan's skill in defeating you depends on the number of senseless scenes he can thrust into your mind. Your skill in defeating Satan depends on the number of senseless scenes you can ignore. Satan keeps a man under compulsive attention to the ridiculous. Expose this trick by making a list of your own fascinating follies as they appear. You might catch yourself dreaming about a giant cake, yourself as a clown, anything absurd. Ignore them.

87. HURTFUL BATS   Malicious spirits never change their nature, they only change their many methods of attack. They turn men and women into obnoxious complainers by repeatedly telling them how badly they have been treated. Knowing that the emotionalized thought can produce the actual condition, they subtly plant fears of ill health into a victim. When detecting a doubtful mind, they swoop down to torment, like berserk bats.

88. BE GLAD You have no need to become anyone at all. You have no need to become someone who is rich or famous or protected or loved. Just gladly realize that you are not required to go anywhere to acquire anything. You are not that frantic need—you are the absence of it, just as a beautiful sky is the absence of a storm. So don't believe in the false need, no matter how long or loud it howls. You will escape a delusion that wrecks millions. Read this item dozens of times.

89. FOUR FALSEHOODS The devil's very nature is a lie, so that is all he can express. Here are four of his favorite falsehoods by which he destroys foolish believers: a. You are safe by remaining as you are. b. Concealed greed is popular and therefore accepable. c. Feel morally superior to others and never mind where you got that idea. d. You can attack other people as viciously as you wish, as long as you hate in the name of God.

90. DEPRESSION EXPLAINED Imagine a lost hiker in the thick woods who seeks a way across a deep canyon just ahead. At various moments he catches brief glimpses of a strong bridge ahead, but in his panic he forgets it. Depression occurs when you temporarily forget what you glimpsed for sure—the bridge of Truth. Depression over anything is impossible to anyone who has crossed over to the new world. See the bridge, remember the bridge, cross over the bridge!

91. RIGHT HOPE   Beware of anyone with a sneering attitude toward life. He is nothing but a dangerous machine. While pretending to be pleasant and respectful, he silently ridicules any noble thought that is above his ability to understand. His hardness is his hopelessness, for he sarcastically refuses to see the harm he has done. There is hope only for the truly remorseful individual who looks at his past cruelties and gasps in shock, "What have I done?"

92. SHOCKING IDEA   Self-treason. Pause and ponder that idea. *Self-treason.* Think you might be betraying yourself? Self-treason means *to seek empty goals in life while believing you are serving your true needs.* What earthly goals do you now possess? Marriage? Financial ease? Excitements? Honestly, now, are you still scared and lonely, working hard to convince yourself that all is well? If so, let this shock you awake, which will replace self-treason with self-ease.

93. VALUABLE VIEWS   Those who want to see will be generously rewarded by a superb spiritual law: *A lower glimpse into hell will be equalled by a higher glimpse into Heaven.* It is like peering through a powerful telescope, seeing the same distance down into the dark valley as you see up the sunny mountain. So a calm study of hellish human ways is essential to personal rescue. But to avoid self-righteousness, you must look at hell first. Heaven follows.

94. TWO QUESTIONS   Use this exercise to turn on the inner light. As you go through your day, interrupt your thoughts to ask yourself, "What is my negative state right now?" Name what you observe, perhaps anger, worry, gloom, envy. Next ask yourself, "Is anger harmful or healthy for me?" Reply, of course, that it is harmful. Faithful practice will finally reveal a wonder that few humans ever see. *A new life exists far above the daily experiencing of pain and conflict.*

95. NEW OWNER   Imagine yourself living in a home which you believe is owned by a hostile neighbor. He charges high rent, intrudes into your privacy, and is generally obnoxious. One day you discover some secret documents in the home which prove that you are its real owner. You order the neighbor out of your life, which he is forced to obey. With these studies you are collecting the documents which will enable you to own your own life.

96. SICK HUMANS   Still think people are nice? Just wait until you finish seeing the entire horror show. Men and women are depraved beyond description. Example: the devilish degenerate who tries to escape his self-caused trouble by deliberately trying to get someone else into trouble. Think it happens rarely? This sick act occurs millions of times daily, unseen by its victims. Hypocrites don't like an exposure like this, not because it is shocking, but because it is true.

97. HIDEOUS CRIME When deciding to seek the higher life you arouse the enmity of human devils. They want you to stay as miserable and defeated as they are. Having no goodness, they will commit any mental crime to stop your spiritual progress. One such hideous crime is to accuse you of being foolish and disloyal for leaving their sick ways. A demonic man tries to make *you* feel guilty for *his* evil. Don't. Keep your young love alive.

98. HEALTHY ACTS You must admit wrongness in yourself while remembering that it is not your real nature. It is essential to perform both of these acts at the same time. This double act helps you to see that no person is either good or bad in himself, that only God is good. It is like observing your former personal diary floating down a river. You can see it, but also realize that it has no present connection with you. In these few sentences you will find everything necessary for newness.

99. SMOOTH SAILING Suggestibility is like a wind at sea that blows your ship of life into stormy seas. Someone lightly comments that your behavior is sometimes silly, and you sail away into resentment. Someone suggests that you are a chatterbox, and you sink in shame. Suggestibility is a weakness that operates in the absence of spiritual judgment. It fades away in the light of insight, leaving your ship under your command.

100. NEW DIRECTION Up to now, you have written your own life story containing many chapters you would like to forget. But just as an author of a novel can change the direction of his story any time he likes, so can you. There is no need to continue to do what you always do or to pay what you always dreadfully pay. You can write a new life story that grows more fascinating each day. And just as an author knows what his book is all about, you will know what your life is all about.

• • •

Chapter 8
Victory Over Harmful Forces
Part I

We will boldly explore the subject of exorcism and self-healing. We are going to find out all about victory over forces that, unknown to us, harm us. We are going to learn the whole story so that we are more intelligent than what's been hurting us all these years. These subjects apply to everyone on earth. Everyone is concerned with them because there is a very definite connection between the dark forces and everyone. No one can escape a connection with them.

Now, since you have up until now had a contract with suffering, I now tell you to tear it up. You've signed one, obviously, because you're living under it. You've accepted its terms and you follow every point as if you are forced to follow it. Tear it up. Get rid of it. From this point on you are no longer bound by its terms, and that is a fact. Accept the fact.

Now as we boldly explore these subjects, you must become aware as I'm giving you these liberating facts that these very forces that we are investigating are active in trying to keep themselves hidden. They don't want you to know about them. They want to stay hidden so they can continue to control you and to hurt you as they already have in the past. I want you to know that if you can see resistance in you right now, all you have to do is be willing to not resist anymore. You can't fight that resistance by yourself but you can ask Truth to give you the willingness to yield to Truth itself. That is what defeats what has been hurting you, yielding to the Truth, which then does the work for you.

So, you are very vitally involved in what is going on here right now. Isn't it nice to know, that you are involved in your own rescue, that what is being received by you, can then turn into a life in Light. Think of that phrase: *a life in Light*. That isn't your case now, is it, with so many captivities, so many blows, so many anxieties? Ah, all that will change to where the Light is all there is for you.

We're going to start with some definitions:

Possession - You've seen and heard the word before. What is possession? We're going to simplify everything. There's no need to say ten thousand words. We can get right to the point and if you want to understand, you will understand.

For a human being to be possessed, it means that he has been captured and controlled by a harmful force which he can't expel. That's possession! It's taken over his life, taken over his voice and the way he walks, the way he acts out in the world, the way he feels. Possession simply means that a human being, man or woman has been taken over by something that is wrong for him. Ah, let's put it a little stronger.

He's been taken over by something that actually hates him and wants to destroy him. You've seen this, where someone has been taken over and the possessed individual, can't do a thing about it.

What have you done about your fear of life, lately? Has it possessed you? Keep that thought suspended for a little bit. Keep it somewhere.

Exorcism - Exorcism means that another force, a Higher power, enters the individual and expels the harmful force. This Higher force is in fact stronger than both the individual and the alien force that possesses him. That is why it can take it out, chase it away. I said something that is higher than the possessed individual: you, some-one else. Already this has given you an important clue for you to withdraw from your egotistical efforts to try to be happy. To be happy you have to get rid of unhappiness. You don't know how to do it, do you? You haven't succeeded so far, but you're learning right now how to be a success. The success is already achieved but all you need to do is be willing to take it.

Now, when you hear about possession, a human being possessed, you usually think of an extreme case, don't you? You've seen movies of people who were possessed. Don't be afraid of anything you hear about exorcism or possession. You don't have to be, and with what you're learn-ing now, you won't be. You will be in charge and nothing that is dark and hostile can affect you.

But I want you to know that possession is a

matter of degree. Now just set aside for a minute all these horrible cases of complete control and domination, where an individual man or a woman turns into a human demon, screaming and hollering, doing strange, weird, devilish things. Set that aside for a minute. And I want you to set it aside for your sake, for your health. I want you to think of possession as a very common, ordinary thing, which it is.

That is the last thing that these hostile forces want you to know. They want you to think that all you have to do is go to a movie or read a book about demon possession and that's what it's all about. Oh no! We are beginning to be far more intelligent than that because we want something right for ourselves. And you know, when you can't control your temper, you know you are possessed. If you don't know it, then you must admit it right now.

You see, it's a matter of degree. That's the extreme case, where the person is screaming like a madman. But we cover it up and may not show it to others. We don't show it to ourselves either. But remember right now and never forget that every human being on earth is possessed. Something has got into them. What do you think is causing all the heartache? Something is doing that. What is doing that is something that is the enemy of you, of mankind, of all that's good and decent. As you become truly spiritually-minded, with this increased spiritual knowledge of light and life, then equal to that will be your knowledge of the absolute viciousness of human beings. They are indeed possessed and have nothing to give you but that, which is why dissociation from the masses of humanity is an essential thing for you to put first in your inner studies.

Now evil forces, foreign agents, have a way of taking over. I'm going to show you the exact, precise steps by which you lose control of yourself, by which you become afraid of life, feel hard, bitter and left out, utterly confused about everything—so that you don't know how to think and your mind goes crazy. You know your mind goes crazy. I'm going to show you how it happens to you. When you see how it happens, you can reverse the process and stop it from happening. This is very practical—oh, how practical. You can put it into practice, and I hope you already have by being alertly attentive and wanting a life of Light rather than a life of darkness. Now follow this so you see it happening today and tomorrow.

The first thing a foreign agent does—that wicked, evil, insidious force—is to give you an attractive temptation. They present the dazzling goods in front of you, it could be anything. See, they know what you want, they know what your weaknesses are and they put the whole package together. They are not stupid as far as what you want is concerned. They are totally stupid in another way, by the way. Anyone who does not live in the Light is stupid. Everyone who lives in the dark is stupid.

First, they present to you a person, a thought, an opportunity, put it in front of you and say, "This will be good for you." They know what you think and how you think. They say, "Take this and you will be happy." Temptation, ah, that's where you stop them right there. Only a wrong part of you can ever be tempted, therefore if you are good inside they can't tempt you. No one can tempt what is good in you, only what is bad. See how important it is for you to become good as fast as possible?

When the temptation comes and a human being is so asleep, so foolish, utterly egotistical, always wandering around in his own thoughts instead of paying attention to goodness and to Truth. When a person yields to the temptation, there is entrance. That's the second step. First temptation, then entrance.

You'll see how true what I'm telling you is, by noticing the next time you are taken over by wrath, fury, anger, irritation. You watch these steps. They are there and you can stop them right at the start, if you want. They enter you and then they begin to lie to you all the more now that they've gained entrance. Now they want to stay there. The anger wants to continue and you look for more excuses to stay angry and you've fallen right into their trap. And now the possession becomes more and more complete. And in extreme cases, the individual falls for it and the possession comes to the point where a person is called insane, a madman, hysterical, crazy. Use any terms you want, but when possession gets that far, that's what happens to the individual.

It's one, two, three: temptation, entrance, possession. You stop them at the start. It is within your power because you now have the knowledge of how they took you over and made you depressed this morning. How many were depressed this morning? How many were angry today? How many feel that no one likes you? Well, I'll say it. How many of you know why they don't like you? *(Laughter)* All right. They enter and they take over. Reverse the process. Don't let them put a foot in the door to begin with, by staying awake, by *not* thinking that they are friends. And every time you yield to the idea that this is a horrible world in which you are the victim of everyone, you have yielded to temptation because you're ignorant. In Reality, you are not the victim of anything. But if you are, it's because you choose to be. You let enough of these hideous forces enter, take you over, talk through you, walk through you, act through you, feel through you, respond through you. When you let them take you over, you are gone. You don't have to do that. Everything that is necessary for you to know about evil forces, evil spirits, can be known. We are starting right now to get some preliminary points.

And here is an illustration to continue on with our daring expose. Oh, I tell you, you will start to be firm and tough and daring. This firmness will be a permanent part of you. You won't have to think about it. You won't have to hold it in place. The knowledge, the spirit, the wisdom that you have permitted to come, will be your strength in the face of every temptation.

The Light can never be tempted to fall, to turn into darkness. Light can only be Light all the time. And when you are that Light, darkness has no chance at all. Oh, how wise you will be. You can look at a crowd of people and know absolutely everything about every single one of them. Yes! You will know their fundamentals. You will know how afraid they are, how tricky they are, how weak they are while pretending to be strong. You'll know their anxieties, how they feel bitter, how they feel cheated. Because you found out that that's the way *you* were. You were possessed. You went through the healing, the exorcism. Now you can look at anyone out there who is possessed and you can say— without vanity, without conceit, of course, but from the Light itself—"I know everything about you because I used to be you."

You understand that, don't you? You used to be that person. All you could do was argue when something came up, idiotic arguments and fights. You didn't know you were foolish at the time, did you? Now you know and out of that knowledge you know everything about every other human being. Oh, will that cause you to keep your distance, psychologically and spiritually. Not because you're afraid but because you're wise and you're already complete. You know they're not going to give you anything. What do they have to give you but what they are. You don't want what they are any more than what you used to be. You didn't want that and you got rid of it.

Here is an illustrative story. There was a wretched place and this wretched place was ruled over by witch doctors. These witch doctors told the people that even though this is a wretched place just now, listen to us and we'll boil a brew of some kind that will solve all the problems and we'll all be happy. And so they boiled their brews. You'll understand what we're talking about. They said, "As soon as we pass certain social laws, we'll all be happy. As soon as we change the social structure in some other way, as soon as science gives us some more answers, we'll all be happy. We're wretched now but tomorrow we'll be happy."

Because the people were easily tempted, because they listened to the voice of folly instead of trying to understand for themselves why they were wretched, they listened to the witch doctors. They drank the brew and they stayed unhappy and wretched. Secretly they hated each other and clawed at each other, but on the surface they appeared to be nice because they wanted things from each other, just like the society we live in. The witch doctors also told them this. They said, "On the other side of the mountain is another village which is called *the bad place*. You see, this is the good place. We're unhappy but we're good people. We're righteous. We're right, they're wrong. Those wicked people over in the bad place over there hate you. They are your enemy."

The witch doctors were smart enough to know what society as a whole doesn't know, that lost people always need someone to hate. This is where the devil, the dark forces, find lots of work to do and lots of willing victims. So, they told all the lost people, "Get rid of your frustrations by hating people over there." Now, do you follow this? Do you see how this is what the world does? You're supposed to hate the enemy nation, the neighbor down the street, another group, another class that doesn't think or look like you do. You're supposed to hate them and give them something to hate. And the possession, the hatred, the violence and the sickness is complete.

Remember that from the start of this session, we've vowed to tear up the evil contract. We're not going to have anything more to do with that. You are to learn how to do that. Obey what you're hearing so you won't any longer obey what has been wrongly planted in you, that you didn't know was planted in you.

A few people from this wretched village visited the other place and they found out that the exact opposite was true. There were good people over there and their own village was the bad place. That was the good place. They didn't fight, they didn't hate over there. They lived from sunny principles and they enjoyed each other's company because they were healthy.

When you are healthy spiritually and mentally you enjoy everybody on earth, as wicked as they are. Do you understand what that means? You enjoy them by staying away from them! *(Laughter)* You know better. Being whole and complete, you know whether or not to talk to a person, to approach that woman or not. In other words, your score is one hundred percent because you are one hundred percent whole because you practice self-exorcism and self-healing until you attain that very desirable state. Very few people ever attain this state, but you are going to be different. You're going to be unique.

So a few people moved to the other place and they did what was necessary. When you see people who prefer darkness to light, the only sensible, spiritual thing to do is to leave them alone. Don't go around them, don't hang around. It's not necessary. To do this however, you have to be experimentally bold in another way. You have to dare to bear your own company. Does that scare you a little bit? Well, aren't you doing everything to escape your own thoughts, your own emotional outbursts? Aren't you doing everything to avoid what is going on in there because you don't know what to do about it? See, you're afraid that if you see yourself as you are, you won't know what to do next.

Courage, bravery, boldness. You must face yourself being possessed and *not know what to do next*. It is essential that you be without your intelligence, your action, your choices. It is essential that you see this temper that possesses you and the sourness and hardness. See it and have no plan of action at all. This means the absence of you, the breaking of the possession, self-exorcism, which means that you will be without yourself. This is the whole purpose of life, so that you can be without the old nature. And this will in turn welcome the new.

You've seen the movies with a woman in bed and Dracula comes over and leans over her, getting closer and closer to her. You almost know what she's going to do, don't you? She's going to reach for and hold up the cross and Dracula is going to put his cape up over his eyes and back away and leave. This is symbolic. This is good to understand that. It's something that can happen to you. You can do that very same thing. This is information that you are hearing and acquiring about the Light. Oh, yes, Dracula couldn't stand Light either, could he? When he gets near the Light, he faints and falls on the floor. The Light that you are acquiring causes all

Dracula-like spirits, foreign agents who are trying to possess you, to go away. Ah, now that woman of herself couldn't push Dracula away, could she? He was stronger than her human personality, wasn't he? See, we're not talking about your surface self having any power at all because it doesn't have. Any time you name yourself you are naming someone who is nothing but weakness, who is always a victim, who will always fall prey to the temptation. It comes along and says, "Let me come in and I'll give you a good time." You even think that the misery the devil causes is a good time. That's all you've ever known.

The Light that you are acquiring is pure, one hundred percent power. Here is your part. The woman knew enough to hold up the symbol that chased away Dracula. You must know enough to do something too. What you must know is to permit the knowledge to turn into *Being*. The knowledge will turn into Being as you see that knowledge is only knowledge and not Being itself. Being is power, *real* power. You now take words as being effective. They are not effective. The signpost INDIANA 80 MILES is not the state of Indiana. The signpost is just the signpost. If you take yourself as being in Indiana when you see the signpost, you'll never know Indiana but you'll live in imagination that you do. You'll even think that you're standing on the banks of the Wabash far away. *(Laughter)*

When you make room for the truly valuable

by your surrender to Truth, when you make space for it, only Truth, Light, Goodness can enter. Nothing else. Think about that. Isn't that one of the most encouraging thoughts you've heard in a long time? Because you don't want to be possessed anymore, because you want self-healing, your sincere self-invitation makes room. Darkness can't enter that room because your sincerity is already the symbol, the Light that pushes it away. The room, therefore, is reserved only and always for what is good for you.

Even though you don't understand it and this is an important point, don't you dare judge what God's goodness is. You have judged what the dark forces are. You have judged what you call their "goodness" and their goodness has turned out to be badness for you. You have suffered from your wrong judgment because you thought you had right judgment. You, the surface nature, the invented personality, the self-glorified self can never have right judgment. The abandonment of your judgment is necessary, therefore, so that you can have right judgment. Then that right judgment tells you, "Never judge what God says is good."

Do you know what will happen then? With your own eyes, when you're seated in this empty room and you wonder what is going to come in, you refuse to identify what should come in. You used to do that and you invited in hostile spirits. You invited in psychological criminals and they came in and they robbed from you. They stole from you, they hurt you, they beat you and they put you in ropes. You know what I'm talking about. It happened to you inwardly, didn't it? But you stand there in the room and you just wait. That's all you do is wait. You'll be so tempted to try to tell God what he should bring into the room. You're not really even talking to God anyway. You think you are. The absence of your usual self-possessed, unself-possessed self, the absence of the negative self is the silence by which you do not put out a false invitation.

Then the room is filled! Then the room is filled with something that is absolutely original to you, new to you because it's not part of what you used to be. Now you have this true discernment in which what you see and feel is known by you not just created by you with your own mind. I have given you something that you must experience personally. All this work on exorcism and self-healing will reveal it to you.

You know the phrase we had earlier? You don't have to create anything. You just have to let it be revealed. This is a very difficult point for people to understand. You're so absolutely sure that you must save yourself, and until that delusion goes you will never be saved. You will be saved when the delusion that you must save yourself finally disappears. Your rescue, your salvation, the new place will be entirely different from what you thought in your imagination it would be. You thought it would be something that would support your egotism, for example. You see that it isn't that, which is a shock.

After the storm comes the rainbow. You are new, not with yourself, but with a something that is above yourself. That is the final stage of exorcism, of being healthy, of being pure, of not being a victim of yourself anymore. The Light is all you need, and now you have the first steps for walking toward it. Do so.

• • •

Victory Over Harmful Forces
Part II

Mental pain can just as easily drive a man sane as drive him crazy. Now isn't that a nice opening thought to start the day with? See, you thought you were a permanent victim of your own falsely operating mind. Unknown to yourself, you have given up to these alien forces, dark spirits. You have surrendered to them without knowing that you have. And your fear of them is what keeps them alive. They have no energy outside of what your mechanical reactions give them because they are mechanical, not conscious.

You can use pain to drive yourself sane by being conscious toward the mechanical, by recognition that the only force they have is your meek surrender to them. When you wake up, when you surrender to Truth, that very surrender is what gives you victory over mechanical forces that have invaded and taken you over, whether it's a minor irritation one day or a very severe emotional, hysterical crisis the next day.

You see, humanity has the wrong enemy. People think the enemy is past problems or lack of money. That's what you think. What you falsely assume is that the enemy is your loneliness. The enemy is the fact that you don't have friends or someone who says, "I love you." You have the wrong enemy. I'm going to tell you who the real enemy is. You must always remember it, because the enemy doesn't want you to know who the enemy really is.

The real enemy is your persistent ignorance of the difference between night and day. Night represents darkness, evil, sickness, unhealth. Day represents consciousness, light, happiness, brightness, lightness, a nice cheerful going through life in charge of the world because you're in charge of yourself. Note well that you have the wrong enemy. Noticing that, you will see who the real enemy is because as you learn about the night, you equally learn about the day. If you study the day, you learn about the night. The study of one part makes you an expert on the other part. So, the more you learn about darkness the more you'll know about light. The more you know about your own possession by malicious forces the more you will understand the way to dismissing them through the invitation to the Light.

One marvelous, beautiful day will be a turning point for you. You will look out at the world and do something different than you used to do. I want you to remember right now various mistakes you make toward observing the exterior world of people, events, money, excitement or entertainment. Just now you look out and, for example, you see someone whom you envy for one reason or another. They're wealthy, they're nice-looking, they're successful, they have lots of exciting entertainments and activities. You look out at that person and if you are alert, if the sentry is awake, standing there, you will see a flash of envy, of feeling cheated.

Ah, that's a good one. I wonder how aware you are of how often the false message comes from false voices saying that you've been cheated out of the good things of life and someone else has more advantage than you have. When you see that right within your own self is the envy of someone else, when you understand that and go all the way to the end with it, you will make this marvelous silent declaration to that man or woman, "I wouldn't be in your shoes for the entire universe." You're saying it from the Spirit of Truth. You understand that you know it. *That* is living from the Light. That is living from something that is *not* who you used to be. You are a new person now. Your nature is different. Your nature is changed and that nature, which is spiritual, has everlasting conquest over all your envies looking out at the world and wishing that you had something that someone else has.

Now we're going to look very closely into the difference between day and night, into seeing that there is a difference in the first place. Now it's blurred, isn't it? You don't know right from wrong. You say you do and you think you do. You know your preferences. But how many times have you chosen things that are bad for you that turned out bad? That proves that you don't know the difference between what is good for you and what is bad.

Remember when we talked about possession being very subtle in entering you? First it tempts you, then it makes entrance, then it takes over. Here are several ways for you to stop it right in its tracks. Notice for instance that the Light never approaches darkness. The Light, being light, has nothing in common with darkness so it wants nothing from it. The Light is unique, all alone, independent, supreme, dominant—it has dominion over everything.

Darkness on the other hand has a sick compulsion to approach Light with one aim in mind: to attack in a thousand ways. The darkness is absolutely compelled to try to make contact. It must try to sneak in some way because it gets its false mechanical life from attacking consciousness, but it always loses. When darkness attacks Light and loses, it gets the thrill of a false feeling of life out of being defeated, and that is its eternal destiny.

Do you want a different destiny? Understand everything we've talked about, including this last point, which is enormous. You'll understand so many things if you see right now that Light never approaches darkness, does not want to, does not have anything to do with it and has no interest in it. Darkness has a psychopathic, evil interest in Light, with the purpose of trying to put it out. Just try to put out the sun! It can't happen. But again, in a little bit of summary, when darkness is rebuked by Light, is knocked down by it, is sent away by Light, its own self-pity and its own tears becomes its temporary feeling of life. Then, because the devil is always in torment, the next day it has to come back and do the same thing again. Stated in another way, badness must attack goodness. Goodness has no compulsion to do anything with badness except to ignore it, to leave it alone. Light then lives its own happy, independent life.

Here are some facts about invading aliens, dark forces. First, remember one of the most important facts for you to get into your mind and to watch out for is that evil, tempting forces, malicious spirits are *always in disguise*. Look, they have sly knowledge of what you want. They know the entrances into you. They know where they can tempt you and so *they will always come under the guise of being on your side*. Friendly, smiling, appearing profound, they want you to think that they know what they are talking about. They have made their choice and once they have made their choice to follow a false prophet, to really follow the false voices inside of them, *you* with that small amount of light, just a bit of candlelight, can have nothing to do with their darkness.

Now don't forget the point. They are going to try to approach you. All darkness is going to try to approach you and call itself light. They are going to try to extinguish the little bit of light you have in there. Your chance is to know that the Truth itself offers pure and permanent exorcism over whatever evil possesses you. This is your chance. If you go away from the Light you have no chance. But you won't know you have no chance because you have been so hardened in your phony self-images of being someone who knows better than Truth, knows better than God. You and your self-deception know better.

You won't dare to look in the mirror and see your own face because you're afraid of what you see. You turn away from the mirror, away from what you see inside of yourself. You won't want to see it. Too bad for you. You should be so delighted that you can be all alone with the Truth. When you are all alone with Truth you're not alone at all. You don't have to follow anyone but the Truth itself. Then you increase the Light.

Then when anyone comes along, whether as a person or in a book, and says they know the Truth, you will know whether they are telling the truth or not. You will know because your own

Truth will do the discernment for you. No one will ever be able to fool you again. You'll be fool-proof. You'll be very wise and you won't even have to think about it. You'll see that man, you'll see that book, you'll see them coming at a distance and in one glance, one flash of light, you'll know everything about them. No thought is involved, no labor, no looking at them and saying, "I wonder if he's telling the truth or not?" You will know because you already have the freedom of Truth inside you that knows for you.

Here's an ancient castle of the Middle Ages that's been invaded but not fully captured by the enemy. The castle is symbolic of our physical and psychic self. Here's the enemy which has broken through. The dark forces on the outside have climbed the walls. They've managed to get in and there's a lot of fighting on the inside.

Does that sound familiar to you? Of course. There's a lot of battling going on inside, but this is still a hopeful, good state for you. If the enemy had total possession and the battle was over, that is the same as saying that the invaded individual had decided to surrender his life and his soul and his eternity to dark forces forever. He had decided to join them. Where there is no battle obvious to him because he blocked it out, the battle became unconscious inside of him. He has so much hatred in him, so much violence, but has very cunningly hidden it from himself.

All right, the right soldiers inside of you are

still battling the enemy that has broken over the walls and gotten inside the courtyard. You are still in the battle. That is, you are still trying to learn. You want to know the difference between dark and light. You want to catch yourself right at the moment that you want to feel depressed or you want to feel exalted because someone flattered you. This is all part of the battle. As long as it is still going on, I want you to know that you are in a position from which you can eventually drive out the enemy, with Truth as the chief soldier inside the castle yard. This is exorcism, this is putting them out. So do not be afraid of the battle. I tell you, that is a good sign.

It's when the darkness goes underground and the individual no longer knows that he is sick, he has gone beyond the ability to be conscious that he's sick. *That* is when it is severely dangerous. If you can see despair in you, if you can see your loneliness, if you can see anything bad that is going on inside of you, that means that self-honesty is still operating. And when self-honesty operates, it can call on the captain of the guards to come and do the battle for you and chase the enemy out, which is dispossession. This means that little by little those fierce enemies you feared so much are chased out.

Here's the 7-foot tall dark invader who leaps over the wall with his sword. Remember how you used to run and hide under a bin of corn? You'd stay there while he marched in. Do you know what you will do? You will stand up from behind the bin of corn. You won't have a sword in your hand at all. You won't have a shield in your hand. You'll walk out there boldly. I'm telling you an enormously advanced spiritual truth. You'll walk out absolutely defenseless, no sword. You'll walk up to that fierce 7-foot giant and you'll look at him, and your very glance will cause him to tremble, turn and run away. The devil does recognize rightness. He knows it and he fears it. He has no choice but to tremble when he really sees it. Now, don't you want him to really see it? That means you have a lot of work to do.

Let's carry the symbolism just a little further. Just now you are battling the enemy. You're crying too much. You're sobbing, you're hysterical, you're feeling sorry for yourself. All that is fighting the enemy, which keeps him alive. *That* is the enemy. Self-hate, for example. Self-condemnation, self-exaltation, that is the enemy, which means you're still hiding and fearful. When you get up with no weapons, no defense, nothing but an enlightened nature, when you get up and look at the enemy, not only will that one turn around and jump over the wall and run away forever, but you'll go to the next one and it will run away, and the next one will run away. This is how, with knowledge, with wisdom, with perseverance, eventually something happens to you by a force that is not a part of your usual nature. This is called the Spirit of Truth.

I want to give you an exercise. *Exorcise with an exercise.* Exorcise meaning driving out everything that is driving you to distraction to put it mildly—driving you crazy, to put it a little stronger—anything that is hurting you. Take a big piece of paper and write at the top: *Exorcise with an exercise.* Under this, list everything you now know that exposes foreign, evil forces as the fakes they are. Keep your writing short and to the point and number them. There are good reasons why you should number them: it separates and makes the points clearer in your mind.

Now, I've explained that the evil forces are fakes. You may not know that fully from yourself, but you are beginning to suspect it. Only a fake could ever want to hurt you. The purpose of evil is to hurt and to destroy. So you're to write down one, two, three, four short little ideas that you have discovered. You are not to set the list aside. Take it out for a long time and go over it every day. Even if you don't want to do it, go over the long list you have. You can have as many as a hundred points if you want. Keep this to yourself. This is your private little work at exorcism, self-healing.

Write down points. For example, the one I just gave you that dark forces are a fake. It's as simple as that. Now you can remember that when you see a human being, a situation, a circumstance that scares you, that situation is a fake. Here's why: *The fear is not in the situation—*

*it is **in you**.* Hey, wait a minute! All of a sudden that strikes you. You've been hearing it all these years and now you suddenly understand that *you* are that enemy soldier, that 7-foot invader. You have created it yourself. There's a part in you that still likes the thrill of being defeated, of being knocked down. This gives you a lot of self-references, doesn't it?

Continue the list. Remember what you've heard and read. For example, after the fact that it's a fake, you can put down, "There's something in me that can still be tempted." How about that? Can you see there's something in you that can be tempted? You men melt if a pretty girl smiles at you, don't you? That means you are not seeing her as she is but as you want her to be. Just wait for a few days, until you get together with her. She's going to be just as disappointed in you and vice-versa. Oh, human relations work that way. The only way you're going to have a good relationship with anyone is to have a good relationship with yourself.

Make the list as long as you want. Keep them short. One sentence is usually enough. Go over it every day. That's your exorcise with an exercise.

Here is an illustration and an example. If you're out in the wind you can feel it. You can't see it, but the wind will push you lightly perhaps in one direction and then in another direction. You can't see it with your eyes. But listen, this is a very deep point, you can see its results. The wind is an example of dark forces that get inside you and change directions all the time. Notice how the wind can change directions. If a boat gets out on a lake where the wind changes directions rapidly, it's going to be in trouble, isn't it? That's why you're in trouble. You think you understand what to do, which way to go. It nudges you and in false obedience you go that way and then it suddenly turns on you and you're disappointed. *Confusion is a chief weapon by which a dark force will keep you under its power.*

Let's see the hands of everyone in this room who is confused. You can all raise your hands. You make your own declaration of independence against that. You just say, on the ordinary level, "I don't want to be confused anymore. I don't want to admire that man or woman out in the world anymore." Your wish to not be confused is the first step toward a very clear day walking in the Light.

Now, I said you can't see the wind but you can see its results. This is vital to you. It's vital that right now and from now on, you're going to look out there and see the results of human beings being possessed by devils. See the results of it. Then you can work back from seeing the results and know there is indeed a dark, malicious, heinous force that is causing people to produce those results. Just look at the crime, the wars, the international squabbling and the hypocrisy of social institutions in which they all say, "We know the way out." And everyone is giving an exact opposite course for the way out.

Your mind can be so clear that you know, that by seeing the results of what they do that they are completely disastrous and false. Then, you won't want anything more to do with them because they don't resemble what you are now nicely, spiritually becoming. Do you understand that? As you are choosing the Light and the sun comes up, the dawn gets a little brighter. You don't want anything to do with the darkness you've experienced during the complete night of your existence here on earth.

As the sun comes up, at your first glance of sunlight, you'll say, "What's that?" You don't know what it is. This is something new. This is something that is in contrast to what you used to see, so you know that it's different. You used to see only darkness. You don't know yet and you're a long way from knowing that God, which is represented by the sun, is causing the Light to shine so that you can walk freely. As the dawn arrives and you get up and walk around your day, to your delight, which is the dawning of a new self, you find that you don't stumble against the rocks like you used to. You can see a rock now whereas, you couldn't see it before in the darkness.

I know you agree with this, isn't it a terrible thing to not know where you're going? When you don't know where you're going there is only the bumping, the falling, the sobbing, the anger and the hatred. Isn't that a dreadful way to go through your life? Let those who refuse the dawn, who refuse the Light, walk where and how they want to walk. You must see that the newness is your newness. Newness cannot be tempted towards going back to sleep during the day and wake up during the night. This is what devils do.

Malicious forces, by the way, laugh at you. Maybe that will produce right emotion in you. Do you know that everyone who deceives you, laughs at you? They are laughing at you as a gullible victim. You don't like to be laughed at, do you? All right. You won't be laughed at as you are now if you know that *absolutely nothing is too low for them to do.* This is one of the most powerful but simple phrases you can ever be given about evil spirits. As the Light dawns and you walk in the Light, you see people as they are, your own relatives, the people you work with. You will see a certain person do or say something and you'll say, "I wouldn't have believed anyone could be that sick." Oh, this is just the beginning. You're going to see someone else do something that was sicker than that. All this time you are going through a number of little shocks.

You can't believe it, but you are forced to accept it as a fact—the evil that was so invisible to you like the wind before, is now producing exterior physical results which you can see. Your spiritual eyes are now seeing the results of what an evil human being can do. The more you see human sickness, psychopathy, evil, ill health, the more healthy you are becoming.

You must make a determination to go through ten shocks a day, not five; then twenty, then thirty, until finally, you have no illusions at all about lost humanity. You know that a person is either in one camp or the other. He either wants the day or he wants the night. You have nothing to do with those who have chosen the night. Nothing!

You want only to stay in the Light, which is where God wants you to be. Be where God wants you to be. Stay there, for that is what is known as freedom, freedom from the whole evil, sick world. That's what is known as living in health. Take the healthy way.

• • •

Victory Over Harmful Forces
Part III

Evil spirits, foreign forces work through human beings. You have never in your life seen an evil gun. You've never seen an evil army tank. You've never seen an evil storm in the sky. When you see something that is vicious, that is hurtful, you automatically see men and women.

Now devil-dominated people know something about human nature that most human beings don't know about human nature and they use it to attack and destroy others. They know something about you. They know that you don't lead your own life. They know that you don't know that your life is your own business. I want to tell you that you don't know that. You don't know how you've sold yourself to dozens of acquired misconceptions, how you have turned yourself over for a false sense of security and having a foundation under you. You don't know where and how you have turned yourself over for false comfort, which you didn't get. You got cheated. You were robbed. You're being robbed right now if you are still living from the impositions of the dark forces which don't want you to know any of this. We're going to expose dark forces right now.

They see you in your present state of not really seeing, not knowing that your life belongs to you. Since it belongs to you, you can turn it towards a high life instead of a low one. You have a choice. You can do what you want with it. People *do* make one of the two choices: Everyone on the face of this earth has made a choice for Up or down, Heaven or hell, Growth or degeneration—everyone including you.

Now, the subtlety of sickness working through human beings is incredibly unbelievable. So unbelievable that you've got a ways to go before you see it with this great jolt that you must have. You still want to believe in other people because you want to believe in yourself. Forget it on both counts. To prevent human beings from delightfully discovering that their life is their own business, evil forces have their sick, evil, malicious weapons ready for you. I'm going to tell you one of them. Here's a real expose. Here's where exorcism can begin to work, where you can be dispossessed instead of being possessed. *Dispossess the evil, malicious forces.*

Dedicated devils know that human beings don't know who they are. You don't know who you are. Don't you say you know who you are. You don't! You've got labels. You've got ideas. You live from them. You live from these delusions.

By the way, a delusion has no power unless you act on it. Once you act on it that means you believe in it and want to believe in it and so you act on it. Now the delusion has power. If you could see it without acting on it and say, "That's a delusion," then you would see through it and it would fade and you would be exorcised.

Evil humans know that you don't know who you are and they want to keep it that way. One of their most malicious weapons is planting self-doubt in your mind, not only planting self-doubt but switching the doubts all day long. Here is an example. You are in a family or social situation in which you think you're secure because you have friends. You have people around that you think are going to love and protect you. Therefore, you have an image, a picture of being someone who is protected, solid. Then the rug is pulled out from under you by human devils working invisibly but with visible results.

When the marriage breaks up, the love affair falls apart, the children grow up and no longer need you, you don't know what to do with yourself. You see, you felt needed while they were growing up and at the same time you resented them and all the things you were doing for your own children, right? That fell away. Now you're no longer looked up to by anyone. You don't know what to do with yourself. You never did know what to do with yourself. You accepted one of the temporary identities of being someone who is important enough to be needed by someone else.

Here is the exact chief aim of a dedicated devil, whether in spirit without a body or inhabiting a body: to get you so confused among the dozens of selves, identities, aims and ambitions, as to which one is real—you know, none are real—to get you so chaotic about it that you will select one of them in order to feel as if you have finally found yourself. You can look in your own life and you can detect right now which ones you fell for. What was it? The nice loving wife, the money-maker who took care of his family and children very nicely, the educated person, the person who's going somewhere.

Devils hope you will settle for one or the other which people eventually do—listen to this— in order to ease the agony of not knowing who you are. By the way, you make your selection based on vanity and selfish self-interest. In one way or another, you settle for one of those. Having settled for it, evil forces will then come and apply the cement to it in order to make it harder and harder. They know that you will fall for the whole artificial structure and say, "Ah, indeed, at last I have found myself. I'm a very devout, religious person." Or they say, "I am someone who's carefree and happy. I have no attachments. No one ties me down. I'm just a happy wanderer around the world." There's the hardened cement. You name the one or a thousand self-deceptions, self-images that you have fallen for. See all this.

Now, I gave you a key thought a minute ago. Evil, devils, malicious spirits know that you are desperate, eager, frantic to find a way to ease the heartache. You'll do anything, as you are now, to push it aside—which is merely covering up with cement—so you can switch thoughts. You are only switching thoughts, *not Being, not your nature.* Before you were pained, "I don't know who I am. I'm lonely. Here I am thirty-five and I haven't made it in any area of life. I don't know where I'm going." That's your identity for now, a false identity. See, you want to be lost. If you are lost you want to be lost.

You say you don't need these truths and you go away and abandon them. I want to tell you something and all of you listen to me! You will never, never escape the agony, the anguish, the pounding, haunting feeling that you have as long as you resist Truth. *As long as you are separated from God,* which you are, you will suffer. That's good news. I've just given you the way out. If you want to stop lying about your inner condition and you don't want to suffer anymore, you know what to do. Isn't it gratifying to know that Truth is a sledgehammer. That sledgehammer is more powerful than any block of cement. It can knock it down. Oh, it takes work, it takes pounding away. It takes you going out all day long and hitting it hard with what you've learned here. Peace of mind, real happiness, ease, not having a quarrelsome nature, that is the result of finally yielding. That is the result of letting exorcism work for you. That is who you will really be, a person who doesn't have to argue anymore.

Here is a story of an elephant which was put in front of a man who was told, "There's an elephant." He said, "What elephant?" That's you. You are hardened in your image and therefore stuck with it, stuck by it though you'll argue that you're not lost. You are, but you say that you're found. I challenge you to try to prove your "foundness" to yourself. You'll never do it. Why are we saying this? Not to hit you and make you feel bad. Everything taught here is giving you the one chance you have to no longer be you. You don't really like being you, but that's all you've got! You really detest being you.

Look at the chance you have right now—and you argue. Who are you arguing with, by the way? You have no idea. You argue with anyone, anything because you like the feel of argument. You argue and say that you know what you're doing, that you've been right all the time. Look at all your headaches and look at all your heartaches. Can you have the spiritual honesty to see that you've been lying to yourself? If you do that, that is one of the sledgehammers that will begin to knock aside the cement. So, pretty soon there is no division in you at all but something that is different, that can hear and is eager every minute to put you in a position where you can hear more. Gradually you'll be ready for higher lessons: kindergarten at first, then first and second grade. Pretty soon the sixth grade and high school and college and way beyond that. All the time you're eager to learn more.

Do you remember when you were in the third grade and your sixth grade brother came home with work you didn't think you could ever understand? But when you got to the sixth grade, you understood it nicely. It is the same way with spiritual education. That's why persistence is so important.

Story time! This story is about human beings who are smiling human devils, that's everybody out there. You are trying to be different.

There was a town and in this town everybody was happy, peaceful, content. That was their original situation. The reason they were happy was because they lived on a plain on the meadowland and up on a mountain on one side was a pure white light. This pure white light shone down on the village and on the people. It had healthy radiations. It could send out peace. It could send out understanding. It could send out everything that was good for the villagers down there. So receiving this white light, they were very happy. They were peaceful, no quarrels, no evil competition. There was no argument and strife, which is a land unlike this world.

However, there lived in this village some very badly damaged human beings. These damaged human beings began to love badness more than the radiations from the light up on the mountain. When they did that they began to plot and scheme. Here's how these human devils planned. They said, "Hey, that white light has control, power, influence over everyone in this big village. We would like to have power."

Do you know that's the first statement of sickness? Power! You want to have power over someone so you can hurt them, so you lie and say you want to help them. They started spreading lies and rumors around town that they were going to give them a better life that would make them even more happy than the white light up there. So they did.

They set another white light on the opposite mountain on the opposite side of town and its rays also came down on the people. But, you see, this was a fake white light and instead of sending down peace and quiet, it sent down a sense of division, it sent down ego-competition, it sent down a sleep state and gradually everybody began to fall under it.

When they fell under its spell, they began to hate each other, they all began to feel cheated, to feel that everyone had more than they did. They got sick. They got mentally sick and they turned into the same kind of devils which had caused the trouble in the first place. They became like their influencers. Finally one day a few of them saw through it, as you have to see through it and not love the excitement of it. When they saw through it, they moved over near the authentic white light and they lived happily ever after. Oh, yes, this is a true, spiritual statement. They lived happily ever after.

Let this be a lesson to you that the sicker a human being is, the more he lives off of evil vibrations. Evil vibrations become his need, his desperate source of feeling. Now how's he going to get it? How do evil people get the food they need in the argument, in the fight, in the inner quarreling with themselves, how do they get it? That's simple. You just go out and stir up trouble any way you can.

Maybe you can notice this in an extremely

sick person. Do any of you know a "supersicky?" Think of him or her. It can be male or female. Look at what this person does. Notice that wherever he goes, he stirs up trouble. Right? He quarrels with someone, makes a remark to someone, imposes himself on someone. Why? That man or woman is desperately hungry. Without that, he can't get the shot that he needs for the day. Without that, he would have no wrong feeling, which is what he wants.

Remember I told you earlier that an unconscious human being lives from mechanical energy? Only conscious energy can subdue it, walk away from it and have power over it. So, here we have the human situation clear and right in front of us. Desperate human beings who have settled for a false sense of self, which means they are apart from God, which means that self-convincing becomes a daily desperation that they have to grasp all the time and the way they do that is to pick a fight. Everybody knows that if you hit someone, they're going to hit you back. If you make a sarcastic comment to someone, they're going to make one back. You know that. Devils know that and that's why they do it. The chief fear of a demon-dominated human being is that you'll ignore him. See a clue there? See your behavior? Not only with supersickies but with any sickies. Don't feed them. They won't keep coming around. If you don't give them what they want, they'll go somewhere else. This is the way it will eventually end up. Eventually, all people who belong in hell end up in hell. That's where they're happy. They're not happy in Heaven. Devils are happy in hell, where they can slander each other, snarl, sneer at each other, very smoothly deceive each other and get ego-gratification from that. You understand, do you not, that the hell we talk about is here on earth? This earth is hell. Would you have the nerve to call it heaven?

I'm going to give you one of the most powerful, marvelous thoughts in connection with this series of exorcism and self-healing that you will ever hear in your life. Write it down somewhere and don't miss it. Very simply and to the point: *The devil can't follow you out of hell.* The devil doesn't know the way out of hell. Absorb it. The devil doesn't know the way out of hell! You can know. You're learning it now. What does that mean? It means this: If you don't want to stay where you are now, where your life is devoted to manufacturing a crisis a minute in order to feel vibrations, if you don't want that, you can sacrifice that. Just give it up. Say, "I don't want it anymore," and refuse. You can refuse. There is such a thing as spiritual refusal. Then you are taking steps out of hell. As you go out, there's no way the vibrations and all your negative patterns can follow you out. A devil can't live outside of the hell he has created for himself. Hell is burning hot down there. You were living down there because you didn't know you could get out. Now you get out and you leave them behind.

Here's the test for you. Do you want to get out? If you want to get out, you can get out. If you don't want to get out, you won't get out. If you're not out you didn't choose to get out. You try to evade that statement. If you are still suffering from yourself there is a reason for it and the reason is called you and your present choice. You can make a different choice. You can get out if you want.

Once upon a time there was an army general who was suspected of committing a crime. He was so suspect that the army decided to investigate him. They sent a lieutenant over to ask him questions about where he was on that night, what he was doing, did he have any witnesses who could say where he was. Does he have an alibi? Now if you know anything about army rank, it's a little bit strange for a lowly lieutenant to be questioning a general, right?

Ah, there's a spiritual application, isn't there? That general was being questioned by a lieutenant but guess what? That lieutenant had been authorized and commissioned by the Inspector General of the whole army. The Inspector General is someone who investigates this sort of thing and has absolute power. He told the lieutenant to go to the general. It was the same thing as if the authority of the Inspector General was talking to the suspect general even though the messenger was a mere lieutenant. All *you* have to do is be a lieutenant. You have the power of the whole universe, which is Truth itself in back of you. You could go anywhere. You can be just as bold as you want.

The general was suspected of a crime. You can do more than suspect that this world is a criminal world. I gave you the term psychological criminal earlier. People out there are just that. What is that to you? You still think there's a contest because you wanted there to be a conquest. You're just a little lowly lieutenant. That's all you need to be. You can be a representative of God and that's all you need to be.

Why then are you still fearful that you're not going to make it? Why are you still anxious over the fact you can't break that habit? Why are you still worried that people might reject you? Why are you trembling over thinking that your present so-called stable life will be taken away from you. If you worry about your stability, you have no stability. When you're really on solid ground, when you know that you're backed up by the Grand General of the Universe, you don't think about whether you're safe or not. You're not concerned whether tomorrow's going to be okay or not. You know it is. You know who you've been taking your orders from. You know that there's something coming into you from this higher source and that higher source is living through you.

You don't have to take thought for anything except for daily life. You have to decide what you want at the grocery store or what you're going to do tomorrow about your car repairs. But you don't have to think about yourself because there's no self to think about. All self-doubt is gone because there is no identity there to think about. There is Awareness. There is a Purity. There is a Knowing and this Knowing is absolutely 100% confident. That means that you, having this new state, are truly confident.

I tell you, you don't care what happens to your business. You really don't care. You don't care what happens to your social relations. You're not trying to hold them together. There's nothing any-more to be held together. All is well with you. When all is well with you, are you going to look around and worry about something that is not you? Know who you really are. You can know, not through thought but through knowing, through spiritual instruction and awareness. To be well, to be pure, to be healthy, to be "worriless" will come to you when you have exorcised your-self all the way.

• • •

Victory Over Harmful Forces
Part IV

Exorcism and self-healing is well under way when you are living from a constant abiding attitude toward the world. A certain specific viewpoint toward what you see out there and seeing others live in a certain way. That attitude, that very spiritual statement is, "You have nothing for me. I don't want anything that you presently have." When that becomes an abiding attitude and you live from that, you also act without having to think about it from that. Then, see if you can ever fall for the temptations from anything out there. There'll be no gain, no contest. You used to lose all the time, didn't you? Oh, maybe now you still lose. The game, the contest, has turned in another direction in which even now there is no battle because you know it has been won and you're a part of the victory that's already been won.

Evil human beings, human beings possessed of evil spirits have one great overwhelming terror. Devil-possessed men or devil-possessed women fear above all *exposure*. That's the one thing they guard against with great fierce fighting. That is where they're completely sly. And they know that one of their best weapons to keep gullible humans from seeing through them is to attack. It is so easy to throw a human being into emotional confusion, to plant self-doubt, and all devil-possessed human beings know that. Therefore, it is up to you to expose what they know and practice.

Right now we are going to expose the tricks that demon-possessed human beings use. When I say a demon-possessed human being, I mean any human being, anyone who doesn't love Truth. Anyone! As I told you, don't think of extreme cases, think of everybody. If you have forgotten the rule, I'll remind you of it right now. *You're either on the side of God or you are on the side of Satan and that is absolutely it.*

If you're not developing spiritually, you are developing into more degeneracy. One way or the other. Now, do you really think that those people out there are interested in changing themselves inwardly? I'm looking around the room. Where are they? No, they're out playing their unconscious games trying to bring others into their camp, so that they will feel the elation of defeat which they call victory. See, when one devil is able to bring a human being into his camp, he becomes elated, which is horrible pain—which we'll get into in a little bit.

Fact. Human devils, everyone who is not on the side of God, can be predicted 100%. You can be a spiritual prophet of exactly what they will do and you'll never make a mistake. A good mechanic always knows what a car is going to do. He starts it up, he knows the motor is going to turn over and then it starts rolling left or right.

If something goes wrong, he knows what's wrong, he knows what's going on. He knows all about the mechanical parts of that automobile.

A demon-possessed human being is 100% mechanical. No consciousness. He always does the same thing. He is incapable of doing anything outside of his very low state. He is fixed in the habits of hell. That is what you need to know. That is what you must explore so that when you see four billion people with their various tricks trying to tempt you, beguile you, there is just one thing happening inside of you, which is recognition. You know what he's trying to do because you have studied and you've observed, and you see how cleverly everyone lies. How skilled they are in saying what they know you want to hear.

Now to summarize, and then we'll go on. Every evil person can be predicted. His actions, his words can be predicted and they will always include trying to draw you into their net to harm you. The rule is: A devil gives what he is. He is the elements of hell and that's what he gives you while labeling them something else. In order to be a true prophet of what they're going to do, you must not have the weakness in you in which you want someone to care for you. You want human love. That is exactly where they're going to slip one over on you.

But here's the point I want you to know. Pain, wherever you encounter it, is weakness. Won't you admit that your pain is weakness? Doesn't suffering distract you from intelligence, from a clear mind. When you're in agony aren't you just shaking apart. How can a person shaking apart do things rightly and clearly? You can't. You must know, therefore, that any human being whose behavior is predictable and who wants to deceive you, is in horrible suffering. How is that good for you to know that? Ah! When you know that, you can never again be bluffed into thinking that he's offering you leadership, love, guidance or whatever. You see beyond his trickery, his disguises which we already discussed. You can know absolutely that that man, that woman, that so-called leader is in great agony and that means he has *nothing* to give you but what he is, which is agony.

The insight into that, *absolutely knowing it,* destroys forever the false power of anyone ever deceiving you and leading you astray again. You must, therefore, start to study everyone because everyone is in that state. See the little sarcastic remarks, the little trickeries they play, the little hints of wanting a favor from you. They want anything they can get. What do you have to offer them? That's what they're going to go after and if they don't know what they can get from you, they'll probe until they can find out. They're always probing your weak spots. They'll carry off anything they can get from you.

So knowing that, when you are worried, anxious, frantic and frustrated, you can see that you have no strength. You have no intelligence. Transfer it to others. Now that you know it in yourself, you can know that it's in everyone you meet. I want to emphasize I'm talking about everyone out there who's not studying the Truth. It is true of everyone. Knowing that when you are worried, you have no stability, nothing intelligent to guide you. You know that's the way he is. How can you ever again follow, idolize, desire anyone? You may want to buy their goods down at the market. We're not talking about that. How can you ever again slip into idolization in the area of romance, for example. How can you ever idolize anyone?

Ladies, I'm going to tell you something right now, because you don't seem to understand. If this ever happens to you again, I want you to remember what I told you. All he wants to do is to get you into bed. Oh, if he can borrow money from you, that's an extra little bonus. He may use you to blab about his big career that's going upward and he's going to take you along with him. No, he's not going to take you along with him. He's probably not going anywhere himself and, if he did get it, good-bye to you.

Shall we include the men too? See, you men also set up the moonlight and roses picture in your mind and think it's going to work out that way. You don't know that your main objective is to get her into bed. Once that is accomplished and after a few times, you wonder what on earth you're going to do with her. You men know that. I know it. You don't know what to do with her after you've had sex with her, do you? How did we get into that subject?

You must know that this is a desperate world and desperation is always evil. Well, isn't it? A desperate car running down the street out of control, isn't that evil? Doesn't it bump into everything and hurt everyone it can? Know that all human beings who do not want the Light are rushing down the road in darkness and they'll bump into you if they can, because they don't care. Having lost interest in their own life, they don't care about your life.

The subtlety and the slyness of lost human beings, human monsters, is incredible. They will do *anything* to distract you. They'll do anything to keep you thinking *about* yourself to prevent you from thinking *above* yourself. That's what they're after. They want to keep you in this whirl-pool of self-concern, self-worry, self-agitation. They want you to think about that, so that hope-fully you will fall so much in love with the spinning that you will forget that there's a way to jump out of that whirlpool. And if they can keep you in it long enough you will forget. Billions do.

The devil senses that there is something besides the whirlpool. He doesn't want it but he senses it's there. The something besides the whirlpool is the bank on the side of the rushing river where the ground is very solid. And you can go from that bank to anywhere else you want in the world and he knows that.

How do human monsters distract you? When I tell you how they do it, there will be something in you that will respond to it. Once again, there is nothing too vicious for a monstrous human being to plant in your mind. Their purpose is to plant evil seeds, hoping that at least some of them will grow up into weeds that will choke you.

Listen and I'll describe to you in some detail what's already happened to you just today. Realize that it's been happening to you all your life. A monstrous person, in order to get you preoccupied with yourself, works constantly on the subject of personal shame, of self-disgrace. If other ways don't work, they will descend to the lower parts of hell to get their instructions for wrecking your opportunity to become whole and spiritual.

Here are some examples the monsters use to preoccupy you: Reminding you that you are old and unpretty physically. Reminding you by comparison that you're not young and good-looking as you might have been once or like that other person in the room. You see, the purpose of this sly slander is to keep you thinking emotionally about yourself, to so frighten you, to so dominate you by fear that you're not able to break out of it.

If that doesn't work, they go on to their next

haunt. They will remind you of your past sexual indiscretions, for example, foolish things that you did in your sex life, your romance life. They will put in your mind thoughts about sexual disgrace. And when I said that, you all responded in one way or another. I know you did, because sex is such a permanent, common everyday thing in the lives of all human beings.

Now understand, human devils, whether they are in you or in another person, will plant these thoughts for the purpose of hoping that they'll grow until you are indeed choked and that's all you'll ever have. So please, do not give attention to *what* they say but *why* they are saying it. Why are they doing it? They are harmful voices! If they can get you feeling ashamed, then that shame is going to be the flood which will cut off even your wish to find something above the flood. The devil knows that most human beings can be tempted to stay in shame as a permanent identity. It works.

You know from your past days after you had that disgraceful experience in sex, in romance, that you were taken over by it for a long time. If you think of it now it might even give you a little jolt. Every single one of you is doing this, whether you're aware of it or not, because the connection is there. You now know how *low,* how vicious, how completely conscienceless dark voices are. *Your knowledge is the first step to stopping them from tempting, entering and possessing.*

Exorcism and self-healing is well under way if you remember what you are told. This means you're exposing how they work and when you expose how they work completely, they know they won't have a chance with you and they'll go off to someone else. They must always try to find a human body to work through, to work into, to inhabit, for as long as they can. And they live forever in most people all the life long.

Oh, what a campaign we are on to stop them right now, so catch them at the point of temptation. Remember, you can only be tempted where you have something wrong in you, not where you have something good. Temptation is only temptation and it can be stopped right there. That is the first suggestion. The devil-thought comes, the devil-person suggests it to you, brings up your past. Have you ever had any evil person bring up your past? The reason they were doing it was that they wanted to shame you, so that they could feed off the shameful feeling.

All right. At the moment the temptation comes, you must remember, you must practice—and do it over and over again—you *must* remember that *NOW IS NEW*. That's it! That's how you counter the attack. That's the consciousness. That's the spiritual reply: now is new. The devil can't stand that thought. You say it and he'll fall down, then he'll get up again. You say it again and he'll fall down again. You keep saying it and he'll run away.

What does that mean, now is new? It means that you know in your spirit, you honestly, truly, right now are not that person who did that foolish thing. That man tempted you and you fell for his temptation. You thought he cared for you, that he loved you. He was just exploiting you. He didn't care for you, he just wanted sex. Ladies, please wake up!

Now is new means exactly what it says. We're going to have a practical experiment in that right now. The time to chase away the devil is always right now. Remember the phrase *now is new*. Now you've got it in your mind. That's a good start. It's an intellectual concept to you that now is new.

I want you now to wish, if you want to call it a prayer, that's fine. I want you to know spiritually that NOW IS NEW. Do it right now as best you can. That's fine. What you are doing is dropping the clock and the calendar as best you can understand this, for just a split second. But that split second, speaking timewise, is enough to let a little bit of the Light in. It is the Light that you have admitted in, that you know from, that little bit of Light *is the new you.*

That dark suggestion, that evil temptation, that satanic accusation that you're a wicked evil person because of those past evils that you did, whether it was sex, whether it was getting drunk, whatever, that little bit of Light is the new you. In that light the dark suggestion, the evil temptation, must stop. There is no way darkness out there can enter the circle of Light. It's impossible. Darkness always stops where it must stop, where Light begins. Think of a big campfire out in the dark woods. Everything within that campfire light is clear, illuminated. People can see where they're going. There's only that light there. Darkness is out there and it can't come in.

This must be practiced over and over again until the spiritual feeling is added to it. This is what is known as daily, hourly, minutely exorcism and self-healing. When the thought now is new comes first, the spiritual feeling is added to that. Then any time the temptation comes, you'll immediately recognize it.

I want to tell you a severe problem. Your greatest problem in knowing that *now is new* is that you don't recognize the slanderous thought when it tries to enter you. The sentry is not nearly awake enough. It is so fast you don't see it, so that it slips by and goes down into time-memory.

Girls, you see a man who looks like your ex-boyfriend of ten years ago with whom you had a horrible affair. You pass him on the street one second and in that one second the devil, who is very alert, sneaks down and gets into your mind and emotions and you are stabbed by pain without even knowing what happened. Then you forgot about it and went on to the cafe or home or wherever. This happens a hundred thousand times over a period of just one year. All the time you're being pained by these attacks because you were not alert, because you were not using this information to learn from, to grow with. How badly do you want to be rescued? That's the whole question, isn't it?

Oh, I tell you students of these teachings, the first thing when you wake up in the morning, find out how much more of these truths you can apply to your life. Watch yourself walk out of the house, you feel your hand on the car door and you go through the traffic, you watch your petty irritations at the light changing. Do this all day long. One thing you'll notice is how often you go to sleep, you forget to be alert. How many of you have done that? It happens all the time. You're determined that you're going to walk consciously from your house to the car and what happens after three steps? You see birds are feeding on crumbs and finally they fly away. Forget the birds. Stay awake in spite of everything physical. You can notice the birds without being carried away on their wings.

You're so afraid that if you do see the devil plant a thought, you won't know what to do with it. And you'll be ashamed all over again. That shame goes counter to your phony self-images of being good and now you're totally trapped in madness. If you don't have images of being good, when bad images come in they can't hurt you, because there's no opposite involved.

You have to know in addition to the fact that

now is new, that nowness and that newness is the only goodness there is and the only good identity sense of self that you need to have. Now you won't want to be distracted any more, because you don't want to go back to who you were. You don't want to enjoy the shame and disgrace of that sex experience any more. You'll remember it with pure memory and you're not going to enliven it. You're not going to recreate it again in order to feel shame so that you can say, "At least I'm an ashamed human being, and I've learned from it." You never learn from an experience which is still hounding you. You can only learn from an experience when it is off into pure memory and not grabbing you emotionally.

Here's a clue for you, for your behavior with yourself and with other people. If you do it once, you'll do it again. If you make a mistake once, you'll make that mistake again, unless you remember—write this down as the grand conclusion—unless you remember that now is new. Why should you remember that now is new, because that's a fact, the living fact. That's the light. That's the exorcism. That is what you need not just to think about but to know. Every time anyone or anything tries to bring you away from that, you say to yourself now is new. And then put your whole day into knowing that from yourself, from your new self, which is the Spirit of Truth. NOW IS NEW.

Look at the average man and you're looking

at a scared little boy. Look at the average woman and you're looking at a shy, nervous, worried little girl. That's the whole world as it actually is. Now let me tell you the real reason why you were afraid, why you are that little boy grown up and that little girl grown up physically.

Let me tell you the real reason why you're afraid, anxious, worried, concerned, nervous. It's because you don't know what's happening to you. You feel that a force, an energy is acting upon you, which is true. But you don't know what it is doing to you. You don't understand the whirling back and forth and up and down, going places out in the world, meeting people, leaving them, going to work, not finding much happiness there, going to work somewhere else. Things are happening to you but you don't know the how or why. That is why you're afraid.

And you feel completely helpless, don't you? Feeling pushed around, you don't know what to do about it. You don't know where to find control. You don't know how to find strength and wisdom to understand all this pushing around. There's no way you can put yourself in charge of all the movements that come to you and all the sorrows and pains that go with it. You do not understand what is happening to you here in this life.

I'm going to explain what is happening to you. And with this explanation, you will see clearly. With this clearness of inner sight, there will be no more anxiety, no more worry. You won't be a little boy anymore, you'll be a big, strong, mature man. You won't be a scared little girl anymore. You'll understand, you'll be mature and then you will never be pushed around again by anything.

Now it's very vital for you to accept the description I have just given to you. Accept it as being a quite accurate description of your life. If you will do that, you can go along with me for the rest of the lesson and you can begin to understand why you are pushed around. You can make a whole correction so that you're not pushed around any more but are in total control.

If you're living from beliefs that you're the controller of your life, which you are, you won't be able to hear what I'm talking about, so there won't be self-healing. There won't be a pushing out of all the dark forces that now control you and push you around.

You must therefore be very honest at the start and know that your day, your life, your ways have been accurately described. Now stay with that. It is good to know your actual state and not push it away yourself, pretending that you haven't been described. I know that I have described you. All of you. Can't you be honest and say that's true. You are indeed looking at a scared little boy, a shy, bashful little girl who wonders if she's going to get hurt by the next man who comes along. Ladies, you are always hurt by men who are not real men. That's what the world consists of: unreal men. That's what we're talking about.

When you become real, you will know unreality when you see it in a human being or in a social situation. That renders it harmless. You will not be knocked around and pushed into places you don't want to go internally or externally. You are now, aren't you? Internal and external match, they go together. You're always finding yourself in places where there's a great deep wish that you didn't have to be there, aren't you? But you don't know how to get out. You were pushed there by allowing yourself to be pushed there, and that is the sorrow of everyone's life.

I'm going to tell you the single most important fact that a human being, a little boy, a little girl, must know in order to be in charge of your life, which is quite possible, I assure you. There is no way to overestimate the importance of what you're going to hear. I want you to go over it again and again, so that it becomes clear to you. It will finally become the answer to everything that now hurts you so badly. Can you admit—let's try a little deliberate sincerity—that behind all your fake fronts is the fact that you are afraid, that you hurt a lot and that you don't know where to look for help. You kid yourself and say, "Well, tomorrow I'll find something different." You won't unless you listen with complete attention and interest to what you're going to hear next.

I'm going to tell you the real reason you are always worried, why you always feel alienated from yourself, why you are pushed around by the winds of psychological dark forces. The first thing I want you to understand is that fear is bad. How simple it is. Now, put some logic into this. You are afraid. This anxiety you have is bad. My question to you is this. Since fear is a bad, tormenting thing, why have you put up with it? Isn't fear tormenting? All right. Why have you endured it, agreed to it, up to your present age? Why?

For one thing, maybe you never ever heard the way out before. You are hearing it now. Oh, we've got a lot of good things ahead of us. No one ever told you. You never went to a place before where you were told the truth. How to open the gate and get out of yourself. It's yourself that you're concerned with. Get out of your own problems. You've never heard it before. You're going to hear it now.

There's so much in you that is tied to fear. You like the familiarity of it and take it as a certain guidance. When you don't know what else to do, you fall into a worry or anxiety or a trembling of some kind, and you take that as the answer.

A situation in the exterior world comes along and you take trembling as an answer. Now you know that's not intelligent. How can it be intelligent to start shaking when confronted by a crisis. You don't understand that you are so deeply under these dark forces, these exterior and interior influences. You don't understand how much they've taken you over and have made your behavior, the often silly behavior that it is.

By understanding the basis of fear, you will finally understand that you are taken over by something that had no business being in your life. And you will understand the great trouble that anxiety and tension causes. Doesn't anxiety cause you to do impulsive and foolish things? Isn't it involved in foolish attitudes? Isn't there fear involved in the heartaches of this society you live in? All the fighting among human beings, the slandering and hating of each other, the crimes and wars, don't you know that fear is involved in that? Aren't you already eager to get rid of all forms of tension and stress and anxiety.

Now listen carefully. If you see it, which it is possible for you to do right now, you will want nothing more to do with what has been hurting you. You won't anymore want to be the willing victim of dark forces that come along and attack you all day long and all night long. You will no longer be a willing victim and that is a marvelous start in itself where your psychological, spiritual NO is growing in power and in intensity and it begins to speak for you. You see, you're now speaking with your own weakness. You're talking from that, and what effect does that have? How can you believe that a fearful no, which you have now, has any strength? You will learn how to have a pure spiritual wholesome NO to everything that you've now yielded to. Instead of you yielding to it, it will yield to you. You will see it walk away. What does that mean in practical terms? It means you're not going to worry anymore over what you used to consent to worry to, because you've seen the folly of it.

And now, I'm going to come to the fundamental fact that I mentioned earlier. In order to cease being a victim of yourself and of life, you must know about this single most important thing. You'll learn more about other people as you learn about yourself. You will begin to be wholesome, to be happy, to be really happy. Do you want to be happy? I'm going to tell you how right now.

You have to receive the following information, so receive it now. You are afraid. What is your greatest overwhelming, fundamental fear: *You fear that you are not your imaginary identity.* That's it! You fear that you are not the delusory self that you thought you were. And you fear that this invented self may some day be seen through.

Aren't you afraid of being seen through? Of course you are. It's one of your greatest terrors. Someone's going to catch you out of a role that you play, and you're going to be shocked and ashamed. You fear that your false, unnatural nature is not real and it isn't. It is not real. But you fear that you will see through it and then you're afraid. You'll be afraid that you won't know who you are. But please, you don't know who you are now. That's why you're afraid because you have an artificial personality which expresses itself in all these horrible, malicious ways.

Your artificial personality does artificial acts, gets artificial results, and there's the pain and there is the heartache. Now you see how we've come right back to an original point. You don't know what's happening to you because this invented personality built upon all your past experiences and pains and pleasures, this artificial personality has no intelligence. It can't see. It can't see anything that is happening to you. It's taken you over and you can't see it. It controls you and takes you into horrible places both inwardly and outwardly, getting you into trouble all the time.

You know that falling into trouble is a habit with you, don't you? All right. Now, you have been living from who you are not and you're terrorized that something may take away your artificial self and then you will feel that you will be empty, lost and wandering.

The best way to illustrate it is with the idea of amnesia. You know what amnesia is, don't you? You've seen stories of it. You've read of a man who was walking down the street and he hit his head in some way or he got a great shock over some sight he saw, and he wanted to block out what he'd seen, so he went into amnesia. In other words, he forgot who he was. He was a middle-aged man maybe, living in a middle-class neighborhood with a wife and two children. There are hundreds, thousands of cases actually like that. And so forgetting who he was, instead of coming home at night, he got on a bus and went somewhere. Then he got on another bus, wandering around not knowing that he had forgotten who he really was.

Listen to this please, because it's so characteristic of spiritual amnesia. The bus took him to the opposite side of town and he got off at a strange street 25 miles away from his home, and he started walking down the street not knowing where he was going. You don't know where you are going. He didn't know what he was supposed to be doing, he didn't know his name.

See how his anxiety and tension set in because he would get on the bus to go to the oppposite side of town where he lived. His identification had been lost in some way and his anxiety is this. He is wandering around not knowing what to do with himself, where to go. And listen carefully to what I'm going to say next. All the time he is walking around not knowing where to go, the sun is going down. Let that sink in.

You see, if you were on the spiritual path, if you'd got rid of your spiritual amnesia, you would have a sensing of the direction of home. Each new spiritual principle that you absorb would steady your walk so that you would feel and know that you're heading in the right direction to home, away from your wandering around out there. You would know that it's getting later in the day and you'd also know that you're heading home and could get home before dark. Not the way you are now. You don't have that yet. This is why you got off that bus at the end of the bus line, way out of the city limits where the dark woods begin. And you get off and you sense and see that sun going down. And you don't know where you're going to spend the night. You don't know what to do.

Carry on with our illustration of the man who has actual amnesia. He goes out and he finds a place, he sleeps in the woods or something. Gets up the next day, and he wanders from here to there, all the time being compelled by something, some power that has taken him over that he knows nothing about, so that he has no control at all.

Well, in some cases they do come to themselves and they finally get back home. But we're talking about spiritual amnesia now. You're under it. You don't know who you are and the reason you don't know who you really are is because you insist on remaining in spiritual amnesia instead of waking yourself up with the knowledge you are being given.

Everything you've heard can be a part of your inner wish and desire and energy, to shake your head and look around and see that you're in the wrong place. And one of the places where you can start to work on right now is the fact that you're in the wrong place called anxiety, called worry, called nervousness. That's a good word. How many of you are nervous? You know that's your whole life. There's no way you can bluff and fake it. Just say to yourself right now while I'm talking to you, this would be a way to get health into you right at this very minute, to simply admit, "I am nervous." And don't say, "I'm nervous because this is a horrible world."

See, now you've diluted it, you've weakened it. Say "I am nervous" so that you can go on from there and understand what we're talking about. Say, "I'm nervous because I'm living in the wrong place internally, and I'm wandering around there. I get on the internal bus and go 20 miles, I get on an airplane and go 5,000 miles and all the time, I do indeed have this apprehension that I'm not in the right place."

Now, I'll ask you, "How can you ever say that living as you now are internally is a right place?" Can you settle it once and for all right now, that it is bad for you to argue with Truth when it tries to help you. Don't you know that's bad. Can you do that right now? You see, you have a chance to work right now. The Truth is on your side. You have a special opportunity right now. Take advantage of it right now by yielding fully, as fearful as you are to do so. Don't you know that fear is afraid of real courage. If you will just put yourself on the right side, that will do the work for you.

I've told you that your chief fear is that what you were calling yourself may turn out to be untrue after all. Face it right now that it is untrue after all. Never mind. Listen carefully. Never mind who you will be when you have the spiritual courage to drop your amnesia. Never mind asking yourself who will you be when you willingly and voluntarily dissolve the false self, the unnatural self.

I direct you to have no concern for tomorrow. I direct you to have no anxiety over who you will be tomorrow. You must simply relax right now and drop all your conditioned ideas, all your false beliefs. Oh, listen to this one: don't be concerned over dropping your fighting spirit. See, all fighting includes fear. If you were to stop fighting, you couldn't be afraid. And when you are no longer afraid, you are no longer your spurious wrong nature, but you are someone else.

Now, I want to tell you what you just asked me. I can read your minds. I know how your mind is working. I said, "Drop your artificial nature and have no concern for who you will be tomorrow." You said, "But please couldn't you give me a hint of who I'll be? Couldn't you suggest it in some way so that I will have assurance that I'll have someone to be tomorrow?" I am not going to fall for that—I see it so clearly—and I am not going to permit you to fall for it. One ounce of error can spoil ten tons of truth. We go all the way 100% and here's what I mean by that. You must be so inwardly relaxed, so agreeable to letting Truth, God take over and do what God wants, so that you no longer have any reservations at all about it.

Don't ask, "Please give me assurance that I'll be all right?" Well, what do you think God is? Isn't God completely spiritual, completely true, completely reliable, completely compassionate and loving. See, you don't really trust God. But, all right, I understand that for now. I'm telling you to do something that will put you in a position where you have nothing but the spiritual life, where it controls everything, where there's no time-thinking toward tomorrow or next week or the next fifty years. There's no concern in you at all over the next thousand years, because you'll have understood that eternity is now, *right now.* That's the reason you don't have to be worried over tomorrow or ten years or 5,000 years from now.

What you have to do is let go willingly, voluntarily. Do it fifty times a day if necessary. Let go of the fearful self which is an imposter. All the malicious forces, evil spirits use your fearful self to live in and from. You're not conscious yet that you have been living with a faker who wants you to stay out at the end of that bus

line at the end of the town while it gets darker
and darker. It *wants* you to remain afraid. Listen
to me, malicious forces want you to remain in a
trembling state because that is what they are.
They want you to be with them because if you
decide you're not going to live with them anymore, they're not going to have anyone to torment.

Who do you think is giving you all these
terrible days and nights that you have? Who do
you think is giving it to you? Someone, something, malicious forces that you've consented to
that you think are good for you. Heaven help us
all. You think that they're on your side, that
they're helpful, that they're necessary. Come on,
break out out right now! You can do it. Look, do
not go along with them any more. See so clearly
that the very sight is your 100% rebellion
against their possession of your life.

Wrong, hurtful attitudes, hurtful convictions
possess your life, don't they? When they don't
possess your life, something else will. Now, this
is very encouraging for you to know. If you completely, with no reservations, abandon who you
now are, that allows a complete infilling of yourself
by the Spirit of Light. That becomes your life, that
becomes your direction. And when you know
where you're going, you can't be afraid. In fact,
with fear being completely gone, your whole day
is filled with a real pleasure. You say over and
over to yourself, and this is a very spiritual statement, that you've left the bus line at the end of

the city, the dark woods. You're starting to come back home because you've recovered from your spiritual amnesia.

All the way home you were thinking joyous pleasant thoughts and your emotions are beginning to join them. You're glad, you're rightly excited and every step you get closer to your real nature, to your real home. Every step you take you get more excited. Do you know that a truly spiritual human being is the most excited person on earth. Why? He knows *real* gold when he sees it because he found out what counterfeit gold was. Oh, is he excited that he's going to get more for himself. God has promised to give him as much as he can take, as much as he wants.

How much of true spiritual riches do you want? If you want a lot you can have a lot. Start right now to want more. Just want more. That's right, that's a prayer, that's a wish. Want more of it and you will have it. Then you will know who you are. You will live from who you are. And you will live that way not for fifty years, not for a thousand, but for eternity. That is your new life. That is your true life. That is what you can have.

Truth is exceedingly close, comforting and strong. Now isn't that a delightful thought to think about. Since Truth is close and strong, why are you weak? See Truth says something to you. It says, "I want you to know that when you tremble, I don't tremble." If you were to remember that, if you would bring yourself back to where you should be internally, you would be right with Truth. *It* would be your comfort. You need nothing else on earth. Now you need a lot of things, a lot of extras, don't you? You've got them. Look at the places you go, the things you think and what you grab for in order to feel safe and secure. Since they haven't worked, drop them and stay close to the little bit of Reality that you've collected.

If you feel afraid, that means you have wandered away. Come back and I'll show you how to do that. This lesson is about self-healing. It's for those of you who are tired of bumping into life and falling down and crying. It's for those of you who feel a strange haunting, an alien force that is there, but you don't know what to do with it. You don't know how to handle it. You're worried over something and not knowing what to do about it, you worry over it. You sense that worry is wrong but it's the only thing you have, so that's what you go after.

You must understand that the process of exorcism, of spiritual healing comes by you willingly letting yourself be melted down from your present hardened state. You are hardened whether you say it or not, know it or not, real- ize it or not. It is out of that hardness that comes all the problems that you have. It's no fun being a human block of ice. It's cold and it is hard.

281

There's nothing in it that's real for you, so why don't you just let the warmth of Truth melt you down a little bit right now. Will you do that? Will you yield just a little bit? You can actually feel the hardness going away. You feel a bit of the pain that always goes with a hard mind and a hard spirit vanishing. You know exactly what I'm talking about, psychological hardness. You're afraid to melt yourself down. You're afraid to be what you are. You're trapped by yourself, aren't you? That's what we're going to discuss now.

First of all, there is a severe problem, that of your present condition. We're going to talk about how to no longer be in this condition, to no longer be you. But every day through your own efforts, you must melt down just a little bit more so that you're fluid, flexible, so that nothing can hit you. You see you can hit a block of ice, can't you? Try hitting water sometime. It just splashes. We can melt down. You can melt down. But to do this, we're going to do something very interesting. This will be spiritual entertainment and at the same time it is very edifying.

We're going to talk about symbolism that human beings have used over thousands of years in an attempt to explain evil, haunting spirits, anything that is against humanity. And the symbolism that people have chosen to use to try to understand evil and dark forces is the creation of monsters of various kinds. You see monster movies and you've heard of Dracula, and

Frankenstein and Wolfman and a few others. Various assorted and weird types of half-human or not quite human. These are symbolic of evil.

Human beings act towards these monsters inwardly as they do outwardly when seeing them in a movie or reading about them in a book. First of all, they're very mysterious aren't they? And secondly, they're not quite what they seem. You're not quite sure what they're all about. You think it might be friendly but it isn't. It turns out to be a Dr. Jekyll and Mr. Hyde sort of thing. And so you are afraid of the monsters, which is the symbolism for something inside.

Aren't you afraid inwardly of something you don't understand? Doesn't Dracula seem to have a strange power? Aren't all the other monsters that you see in a thousand varieties able to scare you? Oh, do you know what we're going to do here right now? We'll get to the inner part in a minute, but just stick to the symbolism outwardly—the monsters with footsteps walking down the hall, the strange noises and the fierce looks and the sudden appearances.

You can learn right now that if you are close to Truth, within Truth, those monsters inside you and outside you, and in other people, cannot scare you anymore because you know how to unmask them. As people do when watching a horror movie, you yourself have attributed power, evil, the force to these creatures, and you feel it in yourself and that's what you like. People like to be afraid. That's another reason why monster movies are so popular. Sitting in the safety of the theater or your home and yet you're feeling fear even though you know that you're actually physically safe.

Now, the unmasking of everything that is monstrous out there can be applied to the unmasking inside. Just a brief comment and we'll continue with the outside monsters just for now. Oh, how brave you can be! Here's the haunted house with a dozen different monsters inside there, some of them vague shapes, some of them ghost-like. And you walk right up to them and flip up the mask and you see nothing. When you flip up the mask, you'll see nothing there, and they will collapse right in front of you. They'll disappear.

I tell you they'll disappear because you created that inner terror yourself in the first place. And when you understand your nature, when you see through yourself, when you see how imagination combined with emotion has created those fears and those delusions in the first place, when you see through it, that's symbolic of you lifting and taking off the mask and they vanish into nothingness. It can happen, it does happen, it will happen to you. And it's about time you went about your business methodically, systematically and very diligently every day to catch one monster.

Now, we're going to be more specific. Oh,

do we have a terror inside that we can begin to boldly and confidently walk up to and take the mask off and watch it collapse. All of you need this desperately.

Now we're going to go inward. We've talked about the exterior symbolism, now we're going to see what it relates to inside our own system.

The monster we're going to talk about which is now very much with you, scaring you, is the monster of being rejected, unwanted, deserted. I'll give a little detail on that. You either anticipate being rejected, which you do all the time, or you actually have been, one of the two. You either fear that you're going to be pushed away by someone or it has already happened to you. Don't you know that unknown to yourself that that fiend, that monster is still attacking you.

Gentlemen, don't you remember that girlfriend? Ladies, don't you remember that man? Was it five years, ten years ago? How many were there? Several, right? You vowed that this is the last time a man's going to break your heart. It happened again, didn't it? Try to think clearly. Why do you put up with it? Think of the abiding fear you have every day of someone disapproving of you, not liking you anymore, rejecting you, not wanting you around anymore, pushing you away.

To summarize use the word rejection, unwanted. You have suffered from attacks by that monster hundreds and hundreds of times, haven't

you? You felt left out, other people got something you didn't get. You didn't get the attention
you thought you should have and you wondered
how the other men or the other girls got all the
attention and good things but you didn't get
anything. And here you're standing in the corner
and they're all out in the ballroom dancing and
having a good time. You can't figure out why
you're not out there.

I'll tell you why you're not out there. You
should get out there eventually but the reason
you're not out there now is because you don't
want to be. You would rather huddle in the
corner with your fear. There is great progress to
be made, by the way, in being right in this
world and working with it, going out on the
dance floor. That means go and engage in
business if you want. Go ahead and be associated
with people in other ways, socially or whatever,
as your work requires it. Go out there and use it
as a schoolroom.

Let's be a little more specific. Let's see,
ladies, if this connects with your experiences.
The lady has a boyfriend or husband, and after
the moonlight and roses has worn off, he leaves
her. She is left without him and she feels rejected,
deserted. The pain and the suffering and the
loneliness is overwhelming. The shock shakes
for weeks and months, doesn't it? And you don't
know what to do with it. I tell you, that monster,
that evil has taken her over wholly. She can't

think clearly about anything. You can see the heartache in her face even a year afterwards.

Listen to me and never forget it, because I'm going to show you right now how to unmask the monster of feeling unwanted, rejected, deserted. You must get this. If you get it, you will never feel that way again, impossible! You'll be free of it. All right, here we go.

That weeping woman who cries in the night is not afraid of losing that man. She doesn't miss that man. Let me tell you what it's all about. She fears and suffers from the loss of her usual repetitious thoughts about the man and their relationship. That's it. She is suffering because of her usual thoughts of him coming to her house at night and enjoying each other. She is suffering because she knows at eight o'clock when he usually arrives, he's not going to be there. Therefore, she cannot fall into easy mechanical pleasurable thought that he will be there and they'll have a good time that night.

I want to stress this. She does not miss him. She misses the absence and the threat to her expectations of being able to escape herself by his company. She was using that man and the man was using her too. They didn't have a spiritual relationship. They may have had one that was enjoyable on the physical, social level, on the sexual level. They might have had a good time there. But what has that to do with them using the situation to find themselves. They didn't.

They just enjoyed each other's company.

All right. So he wrote her a letter from another city and said I won't be back again. Ah, the pain and the shock overwhelming her like a flood. It's her own fault for feeling deserted. She's self-centered. She feels, "Oh, I thought I was important to him. He told me that he cared for me. He made me feel needed. He gave me pleasure. I could talk to him and tell him about my troubles down at the office and he talked to me. Now, what am I going to do with myself at eight o'clock every night?"

Are you making the connection that it's her own thoughts that's involved. The man has nothing whatever to do with her pain. Not in Reality and she has to see this. Every woman who has ever had that experience should be learning this. Are there women who have had that experience? Every one of you, right? If not with a man then with some other type of situation.

So she fears the ending of her habitual, preferred, pleasurable stream of thoughts starting at eight o'clock. She knows that at eight she won't be able to fall into the pleasure of opening the door, and he comes in with a little snack for them for the night and smiles at her. And they kiss each other. She knows that she won't be able to do that starting on Monday night at eight o'clock because he's not going to show up. And oh, is she in sorrow. She sobs and wanders around the house not knowing what to do because she is face-to-face with the fact that she does not know what to do with herself. She has lost her old familiar so-called friendly thoughts. The anticipation of it, the enjoyment of it. Now she has come face-to-face with her actual emptiness.

That emptiness was there before he came. That emptiness was there before she ever met the man, but she used him to cover up the emptiness, instead of using the situation to work on herself, to find herself. That's what it's all about. That's what caused the pain. She looks at herself and she says, "But now what should I do? I can't do what I usually do. The whole habit system is shattered, so what should I do?"

The monster called loneliness and desertion who is right there whispers the answer. And the answer that that monster whispers is, "Miss, I'll tell you what to do, break down, cry, fall apart. Get on the phone and tell your troubles to someone. Try to get their sympathy." He tells her exactly what to do and because she doesn't know that she's been taken over by a malicious force, she follows that advice. And she sobs and she wrecks herself. And she has never found anything higher than her own crying mind.

What can she do about it? She can understand everything I just talked about. If she understood that she would be free. Do you understand?

If the situation were reversed and she had given him a phone call and said, "I don't want you any more," he would go through the same thing. If anyone in that state could realize what we're talking about, all experiences like that would have no pain value at all. You can have a relationship with a man. You can be involved with a woman, if that's what you want. I hope you're very wise before you get involved in the first place.

But listen, if you're awake when you go into that relationship, there's no way that could ever happen. No way at all. Because if you went into it wrongly without being awake, you went into it in order to get a sense of security. You wanted to feel loved. And the slightest hint that he might not come over for one night sent you into a panic. "Has he already grown tired of me? Is he going to toss me aside? If you were awake, you would be superior to every circumstance and every human personality on earth. And if by chance the man should say, "I don't want to see you anymore," the woman, being awake, would say, "All right." When you are free you don't care how anyone behaves towards you. There's no way they can hurt you. There's no way they can flatter you. When you are awake, when you're living from Truth, there's no way any other human being can give you anything good or bad. You're above it. Now that woman has a lot of work to do and the man too, if it's in his case, being lonely isn't it?

Let me go over it just a little bit more. In a romantic situation, social situation, friendship, with your parents, with anyone, you have a certain set of beliefs, ideas, notions that that other person is valuable to you. You think he or she gives you something to think about, something to do with them tomorrow, the pleasant memories and all that. Then you lose that person through any means at all. If you are awake, there will be no sense of loss, because you didn't falsely invest something in that relationship in the first place. You see, a free spirit, a true mind, never would dream of putting itself at the mercy of anyone's disappearance or anyone's flattery. It doesn't operate that way at all. It operates above everything.

So if you have a social relationship, you can have that, but you'll never ever be afraid of anyone leaving you. It has no meaning to you because, having found your true new nature, there is no one there to be deserted. Now if there's no one there to be deserted, to be left out, then how can there be pain? Doesn't there have to be an entity there to feel rejected? When there is someone there, a false personality, a false nature, then by the very fact that it is there means that it will automatically follow its own mechanical reactions, and you'll cry. How about some alternatives to crying. Oh, maybe you'll get furious. Maybe you'll get hateful. It's all the same false self, expressing itself in order to pretend that it does know what to do with itself.

When you sob, when you strike out at

anyone, I want you to know, that is an act. It is
a deliberately contrived act and activity by
which you have followed the orders of a dark
force to pretend that you're still okay, that you
don't mind at all. And you can't believe yourself, can you? You know the trouble with trying to believe a lie? You can't believe it. Right?
Try to believe a lie, you can't believe it at all,
because it's so obvious to you inside. Whatever
you do, study, look at, understand what moves
you make when you feel rejected, whether in a
small way, a little word or a great big way.

Here is a nice spiritual order for you. See
through the series of tricks you play in order to
convince yourself that you're still secure. That
woman, her very crying was her resource, her
move, to try to convince herself that she was
she. On Sunday night she was loved. The man
came over and even brought her a little gift, a
little present, which she liked. And they had a
good time Sunday night. Then the phone call
came and he said, "I won't be over Monday night
or any other night." Immediately, her nervous,
false parts gave her instructions as to what to
do about it. She followed the instructions of
this evil force. It is very evil to try to preserve
her identity.

The woman said, "On Sunday night I was
held in his arms. On Sunday night I was loved.
On Sunday night I was comforted. On Sunday
night I had a companion, I had a lover, I had a

friend. On Monday night, I don't have that. Ah, but I have something else. My identity on Sunday night was a woman who was loved. Then the phone call came. What am I going to do? I know what to do to keep myself going, to keep myself alive. I know what to do. I will become a woman who was rejected, who is now unwanted, and I will prove that I am that rejected woman by crying, by shrieking, by breaking down, by throwing myself on the bed. And thereby I will prove that I have an individual, definite distinct identity after all. I was a loved woman on Sunday. On Monday I was a rejected woman, but in either case I know who I am."

They are both lies. She wasn't loved. She wasn't comforted on Sunday night and she was not, in Reality, that rejected, pushed aside, tossed aside, weeping, crying woman on Monday night. You see, it's all a search for identity.

Study your experiences and see where you slip into any kind of identity so that you can call yourself something, so you can push away the emptiness. Listen to me. Don't feel loved on Sunday and rejected on Monday. They're both false identities. I want you to learn to love the emptiness of not knowing who you are. And if you do that completely you will know who you are. In that higher knowing, you will never look forward to pleasure from another person. You won't have to, you will have it with you all the time. And you won't break down and cry out in anger or in tears. You won't do anything on either side of the picture. Instead you'll be a very poised, very wide awake, very wise human being who has risen above the awful, unnatural, disastrous reactions to life. Nothing will ever be able to touch you or harm you. You will be absolutely free of everything out there, because you have worked so very hard and so diligently to free yourself of everything wrong inside. That is the right life. That is why you are here on earth, to find that kind of a life, the real life.

• • •

ABOUT VERNON HOWARD

Vernon Howard broke through to another world. He saw through the illusion of suffering and fear and loneliness. From 1965 until his death in 1992 he wrote books and conducted classes which reflect a degree of skill and understanding that may be unsurpassed in modern history. Tape recordings of many of his class talks are available.

Today more than 7 million readers worldwide enjoy his exceptionally clear and inspiring presentations of the great truths of the ages. His books are widely used by doctors, psychiatrists, psychologists, counselors, clergymen, educators and people from all walks of life. All his teachings center around the one grand theme: *"There is a way out of the human problem and anyone can find it."*

ABOUT NEW LIFE FOUNDATION

New Life is a nonprofit organization founded by Vernon Howard in the 1970's for the distribution and dissemination of his teachings. It is for anyone who has run out of his own answers and has said to himself, "There has to be something else." These teachings *are* the something else. All are encouraged to explore and apply these profound truths—*they work!*

The Foundation's headquarters are located in central Arizona. Classes are conducted on a regular basis throughout Arizona and in Southern California. They are an island of sanity in a confused world. The atmosphere is friendly, light and uplifting. Don't miss the opportunity to attend your first New Life class. For details on books, tapes and classes write: New Life Foundation, PO Box 2230, Pine AZ 85544.

INVITATION

Please send us the names and addresses of friends who may be interested in these helpful teachings. We will send them a free catalog.

If you would like several free catalogs to give out to friends, just call or write:

NEW LIFE FOUNDATION
PO BOX 2230
PINE, ARIZONA 85544

(520) 476-3224

Hear Vernon Howard
on cassette tape
The Mystery of Dracula
Victory Over Harmful Forces

Enrich your understanding of the advanced spiritual lessons in this book. Vernon Howard is one of the greatest speakers the world has ever known. Discover why people travelled from all over the world to hear him.

The actual recording of talks adapted for Chapters 4 and 8 are available again for you to listen to. You will treasure and benefit from these cassette tapes for many years to come.

ORDER TODAY FOR PROMPT DELIVERY
MONEY-BACK GUARANTEE

— — — — — — *ORDER FORM* — — — — — —

Please send the following cassette tape sets:

☐ The Mystery of Dracula (2 tapes) .... Only $16
☐ Victory Over Harmful Forces (2 tapes) .... Only $16
☐ Both Sets of Tapes .... Only $30

SUB-TOTAL	
CALIF. RESIDENTS ADD 7.5% SALES TAX	
SHIPPING	$ 4.00
TOTAL ENCLOSED	

Send to: **NEW LIFE • PO BOX 2230 • PINE AZ 85544**

NAME _____

ADDRESS_____APT _____

CITY_____STATE_____ZIP _____
<small>XSML</small>